Helion & Company Limited
Unit 8 Amherst Business Centre
Budbrooke Road
Warwick
CV34 5WE
England
Tel. 01926 499 619
Fax 0121 711 4075
Email: info@helion.co.uk
Website: www.helion.co.uk
Twitter: @helionbooks
Visit our blog http://blog.helion.co.uk/

Published by Helion & Company 2019
Designed and typeset by Farr out Publications, Wokingham, Berkshire
Cover designed by Paul Hewitt, Battlefield Design (www.battlefield-design.co.uk)
Printed by Henry Ling Limited, Dorchester, Dorset

Text © Antonio Luis Sapienza Fracchia 2019
Illustrations and maps © as individually credited
Color profiles drawn by and © Tom Cooper, David Bocquelet and J.P. Vieira 2019, as individually credited

Every reasonable effort has been made to trace copyright holders and to obtain their permission for the use of copyright material. The author and publisher apologize for any errors or omissions in this work, and would be grateful if notified of any corrections that should be incorporated in future reprints or editions of this book.

ISBN 978-1-911628-69-9

British Library Cataloguing-in-Publication Data
A catalogue record for this book is available from the British Library

All rights reserved. No part of this publication may be reproduced, stored in a retrieval system, or transmitted, in any form, or by any means, electronic, mechanical, photocopying, recording or otherwise, without the express written consent of Helion & Company Limited.

We always welcome receiving book proposals from prospective authors.

CONTENTS

Foreword		2
Introduction		2
1	The Historical Background	3
2	Prelude To The Coup	21
3	The Coup	23
4	The Aftermath	59
Conclusion		62
Sources		63
Acknowledgements		64
About the Author		64

FOREWORD

The history of Paraguay is markedly different to that of any of the other Latin American republics. Firstly, rather than the imposition of a foreign culture by the *conquistadores*, the native Guaraní aborigines carried out a successful reverse takeover, so that Paraguay is the only truly bilingual country in the Western Hemisphere. Paraguayans, who form a much more homogeneous mixed-race society than elsewhere in the region, are proud to claim Guaraní ancestry. Another factor making Paraguay completely distinct from its neighbours was the existence for 150 years, from the late 16th century onwards, of the *reducciones*, semi-autonomous, more or less benevolently despotic, theocratic communities, set up and administered by the Jesuit and Franciscan Orders. It is perhaps the habit of obedience acquired during that period that explains why the country has suffered from so many, often bizarre, despots since it achieved its independence in 1811.

The first, and certainly the most bizarre of these, was Dr José Gaspar Rodríguez de Francia, whose personality is best described by the title of "*El Supremo*" which he bestowed on himself. Austere, cruel and so frugal that he returned most of his salary to the treasury, Francia ruled Paraguay as an isolated, hermit kingdom in all but name from 1814 until his death in 1840.

Francia was succeeded by Carlos Antonio López, who ruled from 1842 until his death in 1862 and who, whilst no less despotic than Francia, pursued diametrically opposed domestic and foreign policies, opening up the country to foreign influences and trade, promoting industry and introducing railways and the telegraph to Paraguay, making it, in many respects, the most advanced country in South America.

López was followed by his son and designated heir, Francisco Solano, who was elected president in 1862 after a purely formal election. Exhibiting symptoms of megalomania and fiendish cruelty from an early age, encouraged by his Irish mistress Alicia Eliza Lynch, the younger López embarked on a crazy and unwinnable war against his two most powerful neighbours, Argentina and Brazil, with Uruguay thrown in for good measure. This conflict, arguably the bloodiest in history and lasting from 1864 until the death of López in 1870, resulted in the death of probably more than 60 percent of the population of Paraguay and reduced the country to utter prostration.

From the reconstruction period of the 1870s until the mid-1950s – a period punctuated by frequent revolutions, *coups d'état*, two major civil wars and another bloody foreign war, with Bolivia, between 1932 and 1935 (known as the Chaco War), from which, this time, Paraguay emerged victorious, but at enormous human and economic cost – few presidents completed their full electoral term. This situation continued until 1954, when yet another *coup d'état* placed General Alfredo Stroessner, the Commander-in-Chief of the Army, in the office of president.

Stroessner surprised all observers by surviving the relatively few attempts to overthrow him and winning a series of transparently rigged elections, remaining in power until his inevitable overthrow by a coup, led by General Andrés Rodriguez, in 1989.

Brutal and corrupt though his regime undoubtedly was, Stroessner gave Paraguay almost 35 continuous years of more or less stable government, in stark contrast to the chronic political instability which, apart from the brief interval of the Chaco War, had characterized the country throughout the previous half century.

While his shortcomings were many, Stroessner's positive achievements were also considerable. Inheriting a country with only 190km of paved roads, he gave it some semblance of a highway system with 1,500km of asphalted road. He also left the capital, Asunción, of which only a square kilometre, in the city centre, had a piped water supply in 1954, with a comprehensive water and drainage system, and made considerable advances nationally in the areas of both education and public health.

Under Stroessner, the Armed Forces also provided valuable services to the civilian population. Army engineer units built roads and carried out other infrastructural projects, whilst military units shared their medical services with the civilians. One of the most important services of all was that of the military airline, *Transporte Aéreo Militar* (*TAM*, Military Air Transport), which provided a reliable and low-cost air service between the capital and a dozen other locations, mostly in remote areas where such a service was not economically viable.

Stroessner's economic policies were also consistently positive and included the construction of the largest hydroelectric power plant in the world, at Itaipú, with which he exported electricity to neighbouring countries. He was internationally respected for his financial discipline and for meticulously servicing and repaying loans granted to the Paraguayan government by the World Bank and other institutions, thus keeping the currency stable, with a consistent rate of exchange of approximately 126 Guaraníes to the US Dollar throughout most of his long regime. By contrast, after almost 30 years of democratic government, the rate of exchange in 2018 had fallen to over 6,000 Guaraníes to the Dollar!

In this book, the internationally respected Paraguayan aviation historian Tony Sapienza has departed from his usual field to give a highly readable, detailed and comprehensive portrait of Stroessner, his rise to power, his lengthy regime and the coup which led to his eventual overthrow. Having devoted a chapter of my own book, *Revolutions, Civil Wars and Coups d'état*, to the same subject, I acknowledge the great compliment which he has paid me by asking me to write a foreword to it.

Adrian J. English

INTRODUCTION

The year 1989 was crucial for Paraguay. After a long period of 35 years of dictatorship, General Alfredo Stroessner was finally overthrown by a violent *coup d'état*. In a sort of prophetic way, he once said, "I came to power by arms and I will only leave by arms", and that came true on 2 February of that year.

But who was Alfredo Stroessner? In the first chapter of the book, the reader will find his biography and learn how he came to power after a coup in 1954. From then on, with fraudulent elections every five years, he was re-elected seven times, and even changed the Constitution to fit his purposes. He basically remained in power with

Left: Artillery 2nd Lt. Alfredo Stroessner (right) and 1st Lt. Leopoldo Bohanovich in the Chaco War. Right: Military School Cadet Alfredo Stroessner in 1932. (*Instituto de Historia y Museo Militar del MDN*)

the support of very powerful armed forces and the strong right-wing Colorado Party. During the 1950s and 1960s, he was also supported by the US to stop the expansionism of communism in Latin America. But he also wanted to be a popular president, so he started huge projects building roads, a running water and sewage system – first in the capital, Asuncion, and then in several cities in Paraguay – three big hydro electrical power dams – including the biggest in the world with Brazil, and another one with Argentina – international airports, a huge merchant navy and a national airline – *Líneas Aéreas Paraguayas* (LAP). There was also a vital re-equipment of the country's entire armed forces, including gunboats for the Navy, tanks, artillery and a huge arsenal of small arms for the Army, and advanced trainers, helicopters and attack jets for the Air Force. The Police forces were not forgotten, being very well equipped to suppress anyone who opposed the government. As in all dictatorships, human rights were not respected; there were many political prisoners who were tortured and even killed by the regime, thousands went into exile and there was no freedom of speech. The organisation of the Paraguayan armed forces is also covered in the first chapter.

The decline of Stroessner's government, and the coup preparations by the armed forces, led by General Andrés Rodriguez, then commander of the powerful I Army Corps, with the support of the cavalry, infantry and the Navy, and later most officers of the Air Force and artillery forms the centrepiece of the second chapter.

The coup itself is covered in the third chapter, describing the military leaders, the rebellious military forces and the loyal ones, and all the actions that took place on 2-3 February 1989, including the coup's victorious outcome.

The final chapter, focusing on the aftermath, will cover the provisional government led by General Andrés Rodriguez and the first democratic elections in Paraguay for 35 years.

Thirty years after that memorable event, many things have changed in Paraguay, but many others have remained the same. Stroessner died in his exile in Brazil in 2006, but his legacy is still haunting the country.

Antonio Luis Sapienza
January 2019

1
THE HISTORICAL BACKGROUND

Alfredo Stroessner Matiauda (1912–2006)

Alfredo Stroessner (the original German surname was Strößner) was born in the city of Encarnación, Paraguay, on 3 November 1912. His father was a German immigrant, from the town of Hoff in Bavaria, called Hugo Wilhelm Strößner who was registered as Stroessner upon arrival in Paraguay, and his mother was Heriberta Matiauda, a Paraguayan citizen. They had four children, the first two of whom died, then Alfredo and a girl who was named Heriberta after her mother. Alfredo's most popular nickname was *El Rubio* (the blond one), but he had others, like *Alemán* (the German) or *Gringo ra'y* (Son of a foreigner).

Alfredo went to an elementary school in his hometown and was a very good student, and then started at the secondary school in Posadas, Argentina, just across the Paraná River from Encarnación. It was then that he decided to be a military officer, a decision that was supported by his father.

On 1 March 1929, when he was only 16 years old, he was accepted as a cadet in the Military School in Asunción, the capital of Paraguay. To become an officer, cadets had to complete a four-year programme in the Military School, but it was shortened to three-and-a-half years due to the Chaco War, which broke out in June 1932. All cadets were sent to the theatre of operations in the Chaco, Stroessner among them.

Captain Alfredo Stroessner in 1936. (*Instituto de Historia y Museo Militar del MDN*)

Alfredo had chosen to specialise in the artillery within the Army and his platoon was in charge of several Stokes-Brandt mortars in the first stages of the war. He was part of the 6th Infantry Regiment (R.I.6). After his successful participation in the Battle of Boquerón he was promoted to the rank of 2nd Lieutenant on 1 October 1932. In December, he was transferred to the 1st Artillery Group. He stayed in the Chaco during the three years of the conflict, although he was allowed to visit Asunción and his relatives in Encarnación several times. Throughout the war, he commanded a platoon and was known to be very disciplined and organised, which is why his commanders had a high opinion of him. On 31 March 1934, he was promoted to 1st lieutenant on the battlefield, and once the war was over, he received the highest decorations, the Chaco Cross, the Defender Cross and the Medal of Boquerón.

Promoted to captain in 1936 and then major in 1940, he was sent to Brazil for a specialisation course in artillery. On 31 December 1945, he was promoted to lieutenant colonel when he was only 33 years old, and was given the command of the Army Artillery Group "*General Bruguez*" which was based in the city of Paraguarí. In that year, he married a teacher, Eligia Mora Delgado, and they had three children: two boys and a girl. During his lifetime, Stroessner had several mistresses with whom he had other children.

In 1947, there was an Army revolt and most military units fought against the government of General Higinio Morinigo, but Lieutenant Colonel Stroessner decided to support the government. On 28 April of that year, Stroessner commanded an artillery attack on the Navy headquarters in the Sajonia neighbourhood of Asunción, and practically destroyed the place with mortar fire. He was then detached to the south of the country to fight the rebel naval forces that came from Argentina in the captured gunboats *Paraguay* and *Humaitá*. With the help of the Government Air Arm, the loyal troops stopped the advance of the gunboats, which had to seek refuge in Argentina.

Lt. Col. Alfredo Stroessner (first left) with a group of officers meeting the President of Paraguay, Lt. Gen. Higinio Morinigo (centre) during the Revolution of 1947. (*Instituto de Historia y Museo Militar del MDN*)

Finally, after five months of combat, the rebel forces were defeated. Straight after the 1947 revolution, Stroessner became a member of the Colorado Party. He was promoted to full colonel on 1 March 1948. In that year, during one of the many coups – between 1948 and 1954 there were six presidents in Paraguay – Stroessner found himself on the "wrong side" and briefly had to go into exile in Argentina, but as soon as there was a new government, he returned to his previous post in the Army.

On 15 August 1949, Stroessner was promoted to brigadier general (two-star general) and just two years later he was a lieutenant general (three-star general) and was appointed as commander of the First Military Region during the government of Federico Chaves. In 1951, he was appointed as Commander-in-Chief of the Armed Forces. It was then that Stroessner started travelling in order to contact military authorities in the US, Brazil and Argentina, and establish strategic alliances. During the 1950s, General Stroessner received flight training in the Paraguayan Air Arm and even became a certified C-47 pilot.

Getting into power: the 1954 coup d'état

In 1953, Dr Federico Chaves was elected president of Paraguay. Although he was formally married, he had a mistress, Isabel Vallejos, who was a widow. She started manipulating the president for her own purposes and in a few months, Chaves was just a puppet, and therefore Vallejos held the real power. That was so evident that civil and military authorities, and even diplomats, visited her house instead of the Government Palace for many reasons: to get a promotion, to start a lucrative business or receive help with work, money or even health matters. She was the "power behind the throne" and that caused a lot of distress to many people, including the Commander-in-Chief of the Armed Forces. There were even many cases of indiscipline in the armed forces, while different internal groups within the Colorado Party started disputing power quotas. Inflation was high and access to common goods such as flour, sugar, and beef became a luxury. Many products were rationed and people had to queue in line for hours to get a state voucher for those goods. The former President of the Central Bank, Epifanio Mendez Fleitas, a prominent figure in the Colorado Party, was also conspiring against the government and there were rumours of an imminent coup, so Stroessner decided to act.

On 4 May 1954, military forces commanded by Stroessner besieged Asunción and attacked the Police Headquarters to gain control of the government. The president sought refuge in the Military School building, but the commander there, Brigadier General Marcial Samaniego, was loyal to Stroessner and kept Chaves as prisoner, so the only option for him was to resign. The Colorado Party then appointed its own president, Tomás Romero Pereira, as the Provisional President of Paraguay while a consensus candidate was sought. As there were no strong civilian candidates at that time, they offered the Presidency to Alfredo Stroessner. Elections were held on 11 July, with Stroessner as the only candidate. He officially became President of the country for the first time on 15 August 1954, to serve until 1958. He was only 41 years old. In 1956, Stroessner signed a decree promoting himself to the highest rank in the armed forces, General of the Army (four-star general).

The Stroessner government over the years

From the start, Stroessner defined himself as an extreme anti-communist leader, which was perfect for the US Government's national security doctrine during the Cold War. Paraguay was then a very poor country and most of the population – almost 1.4 million people – did not have access to educational and health services. There was less than 100km of paved roads, no national airline, a very poor

Left: President Dr. Federico Chaves Careaga (1949-1954) Right: Lt. Gen. Alfredo Stroessner Matiauda, Commander-in-Chief of the Armed Forces. (Author)

Lt. Gen. Alfredo Stroessner (centre) and his wife Ligia Mora on his inauguration day of 15th August 1954. (*Instituto de Historia y Museo Militar del MDN*)

merchant navy, running tap water was non-existent, there was a very inefficient electric power system for only a few neighbourhoods in the capital, and among many other problems basic goods were scarce.

Stroessner fulfilled his promises to pacify the country, achieve greater financial stability and modernise the infrastructure. He obtained the support of businessmen and landowners to achieve political and economic stability, and above all to attract foreign investment. Therefore, starting in the mid-1950s, his government focused on huge public works under the motto "Peace and Work", which were financed by a series of loans from the Exim Bank and the Development Loan Fund of the United States. Between 1960 and 1980, Paraguay received more than a billion dollars in loans from the American government. The first huge project was the running tap water system for the capital and the main cities. This was followed by the construction of more paved roads, first to his hometown of Encarnación, and then to the east towards the Brazilian border, where a new city was built in the middle of the forests and appropriately named Port President Stroessner. Construction of the Trans Chaco Road was initiated, as well as roads to the north to the cities of Concepción and Pedro Juan Caballero. All electricity, water and telephone services were nationalised, as well as the railroad system. As in all dictatorship regimes, streets, avenues, towns, schools, squares, bridges and even Asunción International Airport were named after Stroessner.

On 4 May 1958, the Vice President of the United States, Richard Nixon, visited Paraguay. The visit served to reinforce US support for

Left: President Stroessner and President Dwight Eisenhower in the late 50s. Right: Stroessner met President Lyndon B. Johnson twice in the 1960s. (*Instituto de Historia y Museo Militar del MDN*)

Left: Stroessner's family in the Presidential House during the 1960s. (*Album de Oro*). Right: President Alfredo Stroessner, the Commander of the Paraguayan Air Arm Lt. Gen. Juan Antonio Cáceres, the Minister of the Interior Edgar L. Insfrán, the Vice President of the United States Richard Nixon and the Minister of Education Raul Peña during a reception in Asunción in 1958. (Tito Aranda)

"their man" in Paraguay, within the hemispheric security policy, in the struggle against Soviet expansionism. Nixon opened a CIA office at the American Embassy in Asunción, and, of course met General Stroessner. Stroessner had met President Eisenhower in Panama in 1956, and would go on to meet President Lyndon B. Johnson twice in the 1960s – first in Uruguay and then in Washington DC – and President Jimmy Carter in 1977. Carter suppressed all military aid to Paraguay for the systematic violation of human rights committed by the Stroessner regime.

In 1958, he was elected for another five-year period, and re-elected in 1963. The Constitution of 1940 only allowed him to be re-elected once, so in 1967, a new constitution was enacted. This allowed Stroessner to be re-elected in 1968 and 1973, but there was still an article in the new constitution allowing the presidency for just two periods; so in 1977, that article was modified and he could run for the presidency indefinitely.

In 1959, a controversial decree gave Paraguayan citizenship to Josef Mengele, the Nazi SS medical doctor who worked at Auschwitz-Birkenau and conducted inhuman experiments using Jewish prisoners. Mengele lived in the country for many years before escaping to Brazil. Another well-known Nazi friend of Stroessner was the former colonel of the *Luftwaffe* Hans Ulrich Rudel, who visited Paraguay many times in the 1960s and 1970s as the Siemens AG representative for South America. The state-owned telephone company ANTELCO used Siemens equipment at the time. In 1977, Eduard Roschmann, the infamous "Butcher of Riga" who was responsible for many atrocities during the Second World War, died in Asunción, and there were also rumours that Martin Bormann, Hitler's private secretary and a major advocate of the extermination of the Jews, died in Paraguay, but this could never be proven. Another war criminal, the Croat Ante Pavelić, briefly lived in Paraguay and even worked for the Paraguayan Police as a "technical adviser".

Left: President Alfredo Stroessner and his Nazi friend, the ex-*Luftwaffe* Colonel Hans Ulrich Rudel, in Asunción in the early 1970s. (Tito Aranda). Top Right: *SS-Hauptsturmführer* Josef Mengele, the Auschwitz "Angel of Death" (Public Domain). Bottom right: Eduard Roschmann, the "Butcher of Riga". (*ABC Color*)

The state-owned *Líneas Aéreas Paraguayas* (LAP) MDD DC-8-63. (Gustavo Figueroa)

In the following years, especially in the 1960s, Stroessner's government paid special attention to the transportation system, with new merchant ships purchased in Japan, the US and Spain, and in 1963 he accepted the Paraguayan Air Force proposal to create a state-owned airline, *Líneas Aéreas Paraguayas* (LAP). General inflation was reduced to the minimum, goods became available in all grocery stores and markets, and the national currency – the Guaraní – became stronger, among many other improvements to the lives of Paraguayan people.

One of the keys to the success of Stroessner's regime was his appointment of loyal military friends as ministers in his government, especially in the Treasury, the Interior, the Police, Public Works and Communication, and of course Defence. His regime's foundations relied on two huge pillars, the armed forces and the Colorado Party.

Geopolitically, Stroessner's regime became closer not only to the United States but also to Brazil, and later to Taiwan and South Africa, and away from Argentina.

In 1959, some members of the Liberal Party and the *Febreristas* in exile in Argentina formed a guerrilla group called *14 de Mayo* (M-14) and planned a series of attacks on government installations. Some of them were veterans of the Chaco War, with military training, but the rest were untrained. They obtained some weapons through donations by exiled supporters, and ammunition, explosives and radio equipment from the Argentinean Army. On 12 December 1959, five rebel columns totalling 250 fighters crossed the Paraná River into Paraguay and entered various cities. The first column, called *Libertad*, with 18 members in three boats, was supposed to seize the city of Encarnación. However, two of the boats were captured

Paraguayan Merchant Navy ships, FME *Yhaguy* and FME *Comuneros* at Asunción Port in the 1960s. (FLOMERES)

FME *Blas Garay* in the River Plate. (FLOMERES)

by a Paraguayan Navy motorboat and all the M-14 members were detained. The remaining boat had to return to Posadas in Argentina. The 40-strong second column, *Mainumby*, landed in Paraguay near the city of Capitán Meza, but most of the group were killed by the Paraguayan Army. Stroessner had immediately mobilised his cavalry and infantry forces, which, under the command of Generals Hipólito Viveros and Patricio Colmán, were taken to the Itapúa and Caazapá area by several TAM Douglas C-47s. American counter-insurgency (COIN) experts helped the military forces on the battlefield. Troops from the 3rd Cavalry Regiment, under the command at this time of Lieutenant Colonel Andrés Rodriguez, were sent to the Caaguazú and Alto Paraná areas, while Navy gunboats patrolled the Paraguay and Paraná Rivers and also contributed in logistics. The *guerrilleros* were poorly organised and under-armed, with no chance of successfully confronting the powerful military forces of Stroessner's regime. The third column, named *Patria y Libertad*, also with 40 members, crossed the Paraná River from Puerto Iguazú in Argentina with the intention of seizing the city of Puerto Presidente Franco, but one of their boats sank. The other boat reached the Paraguayan shore, but after a few days in the forests the survivors were captured by the Army. The fourth column, *Pilar*, was supposed to seize the city of Pilar, but their only boat was inoperative. Instead, they decided to attempt to capture the Paraguayan Navy boat *Bahia Negra*, which was docked at the Argentine port of Corrientes. However, the crew repelled the attack and the attackers had to retreat, suffering several casualties. The fifth and final column, *Amambay*, was tasked with seizing the city of Pedro Juan Caballero, but all its members were captured by the Brazilian authorities in Ponta Porá.

A second wave of 150 fighters in two columns, *Resistencia* and *Libertad*, crossed the Paraná River into Paraguayan territory on 28 April 1960 with the intention of establishing a base in the Yvyturusú mountain range and starting a guerrilla war like that which had recently been successful in Cuba. The *Resistencia* members were soon ambushed by the Paraguayan Army; some of them were killed and others immediately fled towards Argentina. The other column was strafed by Paraguayan Air Force aircraft and pursued by regular ground forces led by General Colmán. The *guerrilleros* suffered many casualties, and some were captured.

The M-14 did not have the support of the leaders of the Liberal Party or *Febreristas*, and many of them were executed. Some 120 were captured and imprisoned, although 42 of them escaped to Brazil in 1961.

The second guerrilla attempt was from a group calling itself FULNA (*Frente Unido de Liberación Nacional*, United Front for National Liberation), whose members were mainly communists and were openly supported by the Paraguayan Communist Party (PCP). The incursions from Argentina started on 13 June 1960, involving the 54-strong *Ytororó* column, but like previous such groups, they were badly organised and under-armed, and had to fight against the very well-equipped and organised Paraguayan Army. The regime response was even stronger this time; the order was to exterminate all insurgents, with no prisoners taken. Troops from the 14th Infantry Regiment led the operation, and by 28 July all 54 members of the *Ytororó* column had been killed. A second column, *Mariscal López*, established its

FME *Carlos Antonio López*. (FLOMERES)

FME *Presidente Stroessner*. (FLOMERES)

M-14 *guerrilleros* in the forest in 1959. (*ABC Color*)

Brig. Gen. Patricio Colmán, a Chaco War veteran, who was in charge of the operations against the guerrillas in the 1960s. (*ABC Color*)

base on Kaundy Hill near the city of Piribebuy. Over several of years, they made a series of minor incursions in nearby areas but due to leadership problems, together with the isolation and hard living conditions in the forest, the operability of the group was reduced to a minimum. In March 1964, a huge COIN operation by the Paraguayan Army led to the capture of not only most of the FULNA fighters, but also the peasants who supported the *guerrilleros* logistically. Very few members of the *Mariscal López* column escaped, with some staying

M-14 effectives after being captured by Paraguayan Army troops. (*ABC Color*)

Lt. Col. Roberto Cubas Barboza (right), Commander of the Paraguayan Army Military Battalion sent to the Dominican Republic in 1965, greeting President General Stroessner (left) and the Minister of Defense, Lt. Gen. Leodegar Cabello. (*Dra. Magdalena Cubas*)

Right: President Stroessner aboard a LAP L-188C Electra during one of his presidential trips. (Author)

in the area for five years. One of the leaders, hidden in the trunk of a car, was captured by the Army. General Colmán himself opened the trunk but was shot by the *guerrillero*, who was instantly killed by other soldiers. General Colmán died in hospital in the US in 1972 due to complications as a consequence of his earlier wounds. It is estimated that 250 *guerilleros* were killed between 1959 and 1962, and the Army, according to official sources, suffered only nine casualties: a lieutenant and eight soldiers.

To have access to a career in the military or police forces in Paraguay at this time, candidates had to be members of the Colorado Party. This was also a requirement to be a professor at the National University or to work in public institutions. All labour unions had to be led by members of the government party, especially after the 1959 strike that was violently repressed by police.

Freedom of speech was very restricted. No critics were accepted on any radio station or in any newspaper, and the only television channel was owned by the government. During the decades of Stroessner's regime, several radio stations and newspapers were closed. Since there was a strict control over the general population, the crime rate was very low. Criminals who were captured by the police were tortured to death or had to spend endless sentences in jail. All judges and members of the Supreme Court had to be Colorado members, and

The Presidential aircraft, a De Havilland DHC-6 Twin Otter, still active in the FAP at the time of writing. (DCH files)

From top to bottom: The dams of Acaray, Itaipú and Yacyretá, built during Stroessner's regime. (Author)

From top to bottom: The Friendship Bridge (*Municipalidad de Ciudad del Este*), the Remanso Bridge (*ABC Color*), the San Roque González de Santa Cruz Bridge (*Misiones Digital*) and the Nanawa Bridge. (*Concepción BlogSpot*)

Clockwise: The Operation Condor leaders, Lt. Gen. Jorge Rafael Videla (Argentina), Capt. Gen. Augusto José Pinochet Ugarte (Chile), General of the Army Ernesto Geisel (Brazil), General of the Army Hugo Banzer Suarez (Bolivia), General of the Army Alfredo Stroessner (Paraguay) and Mr. Juan Maria Bordaberry (Uruguay). (Author)

were absolutely submissive to President Stroessner.

In 1965, Paraguay supported the American intervention in the Dominican Republic, sending an infantry battalion to that country. Three years later, Stroessner even offered to send Paraguayan troops to fight in Vietnam, but the offer was not taken up. His government also offered to allow the US to build an air base on Paraguayan soil, so as to "defend the continent". In exchange for almost unconditional support, the United States gave Stroessner what he needed to sustain his repressive regime: aid and legitimacy.

In 1968, the nation's first hydroelectric power plant, the Acaray Dam, started generating electricity. That year, a De Havilland Canada DHC-6-200 was purchased new from the factory to be used as a presidential aircraft for local flights. It was appropriately registered as ZP-GAS (the personalised registration for General Alfredo Stroessner). For international flights, Stroessner normally used LAP aircraft, a Convair CV-240 in the 1960s, a Lockheed L-188C Electra in the 1970s, and a Boeing 707-321B and Douglas DC-8-63 in the 1980s. Besides visiting neighbouring countries several times, Stroessner made a series of intercontinental flights to the US, Europe, South Africa, Japan and Taiwan during his time in government.

On 26 April 1973, the governments of Paraguay and Brazil signed the Itaipú Treaty to build the biggest hydroelectric dam in the world, with 20 turbines, on the Paraná River. It started generating electricity in 1984 with the first two turbines, and by 2007 all the turbines were active. On 3 December 1973, Paraguay and Argentina signed the Yacyretá Treaty to build another huge hydroelectric dam with 20 turbines on the Paraná River. Construction started in 1983, and by 1998 it was fully operational.

During the long Stroessner regime, four large bridges were built in Paraguay. The first was the Friendship Bridge, inaugurated in 1965,

Stroessner's allies, South African President P.W. Botha and Taiwan's Generalissimo Chiang Kai-shek. (Author)

linking the cities of Puerto Presidente Stroessner (Paraguay) with Foz do Iguaçú (Brazil) on the Paraná River. In 1978, the Remanso Bridge connecting the eastern and western regions in Paraguay on the Paraguay River, near Asunción, was inaugurated. A similar bridge, the Nanawa, was built in the city of Concepción on the Paraguay River, connecting it with the Chaco in the late 1980s. Finally, the San Roque González de Santa Cruz Bridge between Posadas (Argentina) and Encarnación (Paraguay) on the Paraná River was completed in 1990.

In the mid-1970s, the military regimes in Argentina, Bolivia, Uruguay, Brazil, Chile and Paraguay worked in coordination to capture and extradite not only members of their radical opposition, but also potential subversive leaders. In what was widely known as Operation *Condor*, many people who were against the military regimes – intellectuals, politicians, university professors and students, professionals, Catholic priests and nuns – were kidnapped and just disappeared. They were not only captured and extradited, but tortured and most of them murdered, especially in Chile and Argentina, with smaller numbers in the other countries. In Paraguay, there was a huge wave of repression between 1974 and 1976, starting from the first attempt to kill the president by a group led by Dr Agustin Goiburú. All those involved were captured and then disappeared. Troops led by Colonel Grau captured many farmers who were organised in a group called the *Ligas Agrarias* (Agrarian Leagues), which were suspected of being communist cells.

In 1976, a socialist group called the *Organización Político-Militar* (OPM, Political-Military Organisation) wanted to organise a cell for a future urban guerrilla movement, but its members were captured and tortured by the police and many of its members died in prison. In 1980, the last huge repression of the regime took place when the police captured large numbers of farmers. That year, Nicaraguan dictator Anastasio Somoza Debayle, who had been exiled in Paraguay since 1979, was killed in Asunción by members of the Argentinean ERP (*Ejército Revolucionario del Pueblo*, People's Revolutionary Army), which created a perfect excuse for Stroessner to start a repressive campaign throughout the country.

Paraguay, under Stroessner, had very close diplomatic relations with the apartheid regime in South Africa and with Chiang Kai-shek in Taiwan. In the case of South Africa, there was military cooperation through which members of the Paraguayan Armed Forces received training there, and there were even donations of military advanced trainers, at least 15 North American T-6Gs, to the Paraguayan Air Force. Since there was an arms embargo for South Africa, Paraguay acted as intermediary in the illegal purchase of arms through the free port of Paranaguá in Brazil. Paraguay was also a very active member of the WACL (World Anti-Communist League).

During his very long regime, Stroessner paid special attention to the country's armed forces. Anti-guerrilla training was extremely important to them, and the Paraguayan Army, Air Force and Navy participated in many military manoeuvres with their Brazilian, Argentinean and even American counterparts. The United States had two military missions in Paraguay, one for the Army and another for the Air Force. There was also an Argentinean Naval Military Mission and a Brazilian Military Mission for the Army. Later, in the early 1980s, the MTAB (Brazilian Aeronautical Technical Mission) was established for the Paraguayan Air Force. Between 1946 and 1989, at least 1,874 members of the Paraguayan armed forces were sent to the School of the Americas (SOA) in the Panama Canal Zone or to Fort Benning, Georgia, to receive COIN training, including interrogation methods through torture, infiltration, intelligence, kidnapping, military combat and psychological warfare. In the same period, military aid to Paraguay reached $75 million. Equipment was also taken care of through purchases and donations involving mainly the United States, Argentina, Chile, Brazil, Taiwan and South Africa. The acquisition of small arms, mortars, howitzers and cannons, hand grenades and bazookas for the Army was constant from the 1960s to the 1980s. The Army also received Sherman tanks from Argentina and M3A1 Stuart light tanks from Brazil. Later in the 1980s, EE-11 Urutú and EE-9 Cascavel armoured vehicles were purchased. The Paraguayan Navy received several gunboats and motorboats from Argentina and the United States, as well as trainer and transport planes for the tiny Naval Aviation. In the mid-1980s, a large gunboat, with helicopter platform of the Roraima class, the *P-05 Itaipú*, was purchased.

The Paraguayan Air Force (FAP) received many donations, especially from Brazil, with a great number of North American T-6 Texans, many of them with machine guns and hard points under the wings to carry bombs and rocket launchers for COIN duties. Transport planes were received from the US, mainly Douglas C-47s for the TAM, De Havilland Beavers and Cessna T-41s, Bell H-13 helicopters and more T-6 Texans from South Africa. There were also purchases of basic and advanced trainers such as the Fokker T-21 (a Brazilian-built version of the S.11) and Aerotec T-23 basic trainer. The first jet attack aircraft, Brazilian-built versions of the Aermacchi MB-326, the Embraer EMB-326/AT-26 Xavante and also the turboprop Embraer EMB-312/AT-27 Tucano, both of them perfect examples for COIN missions. There were also transport planes for the TAM, with C-47s and even DC-6Bs, and four CASA C-212s were purchased new

The Military Air Transport (TAM) Douglas C-47B. (Michel Anciaux)

TAM Convair C-131D. (Michel Anciaux)

TAM CASA C-212-200 fleet. (Michel Anciaux)

TAM Douglas DC-6B. (Alberto Fortner)

from the factory in Spain in 1984 for the TAM. The FAP acquired the Brazilian-built version of the Aerospatiale Ecureuil helicopter, the Helibras HB-350 Esquilo, which was also purchased for the Navy and armed with machine guns and rocket launcher pods.

Many senior officers of the armed forces and the police obtained their fortunes through smuggling, cattle rustling and even drug trafficking, all under the eyes of General Stroessner, who tolerated such crimes for the sake of peace and loyalty to him. Stroessner himself amassed one of Paraguay's greatest fortunes through numerous legal and illegal business ventures – most of his funds were transferred to secret accounts in Switzerland. His motto was very much "eat and let others eat too".

Regarding airport infrastructure, a new 3,353 metre-long runway was built in 1968 at Asunción International airport, where a new passenger terminal was inaugurated in 1980. Another runway of 3,600 metres was built in the 1980s at Mariscal Estigarribia, Chaco, to be used as an air base and for military manoeuvres with the United States. During the latter period of his regime, the construction of an international airport for the city of Puerto Presidente Stroessner was initiated.

TAM logo. (Author)

The construction of a new 3,353 meter-long runway at Asunción International Airport in 1968. (*DINAC*)

Several armed FAP N.A. T-6Ds. (José de Alvarenga)

Navy Gunboat C.1 *Paraguay* and Patrol boat P-04 *Tte. Fariña*. (*Armada Paraguaya*)

THE 1989 COUP D'ETAT IN PARAGUAY: THE END OF A LONG DICTATORSHIP, 1954–1989

A column of the Army M3A1 Stuart light tanks during a parade. (*Instituto de Historia y Museo Militar del MDN*)

A Presidential Escort Regiment soldier with an H&K G3 assault rifle in a Sherman Firefly turret with a .50 calibre MG. (*Ejército Paraguayo*)

Organisation of the Paraguayan Military Forces

By the 1970s, the Paraguayan armed forces were organised as follows:

ARMY (*Ejército Paraguayo* – EP)
Table 1: Paraguayan Army Organisation, 1970s

Unit	Base (or HQ)	Notes
1st Infantry Division	Asunción	14th Infantry Regiment *"Cerro Corá"* & the Pilcomayo Detachment (later replaced by the 1st Cavalry Detachment *"Gral. Bernardino Caballero"*)
2nd Infantry Division	Villarrica	27th Infantry Regiment *"Gral. Eugenio A. Garay"* & one frontier battalion.
3rd Infantry Division	San Juan Bautista	8th Infantry Regiment *"Piribebuy"* & two frontier battalions.
4th Infantry Division	Concepción	5th Infantry Regiment *"Gral. Diaz"* & one frontier battalion.
5th Infantry Division	Puerto Presidente Stroessner	15th Infantry Regiment *"Lomas Valentinas"* & one frontier battalion.
6th Infantry Division	Mariscal Estigarribia (Chaco)	One engineering company (sappers), 6th Infantry Regiment *"Boquerón"* & two frontier battalions.
1st Cavalry Division	Asunción	1st Cavalry Regiment *"Coronel Valois Rivarola"*, 2nd Cavalry Regiment *"Coronel Felipe Toledo"*, 3rd Cavalry Regiment *"Coronel Mongelós"* & 4th Cavalry Regiment *"Acá Carayá"*.
Artillery Command	Paraguarí	1st Artillery Regiment *"General Bruguez"* & 16th Infantry Regiment *"Mariscal Lopez"*.

NAVY (*Armada de la República del Paraguay*)
Table 2: Paraguayan Navy Organisation, 1970s

Unit	Base (or HQ)	Notes
War Fleet	Asunción	
Coast Guard (Prefectura Naval)	Asunción	
Marine Infantry Regiment	Asunción	Elite naval infantry troops.
Naval Aviation	Asunción	Bell H-13H, Cessna 150, Cessna 206, Cessna 401, Douglas C-47, N.A. T-6 Texan
Navy Arsenal	Asunción	

AIR FORCE (*Comando de Aeronáutica*)
Table 3: Paraguayan Air Force Organisation, 1970s

Unit	Base (or HQ)	Notes
GAET	Luque	Training and Transport Air Group, with three squadrons, one for training (Fokker T-21, Aerotec T-23, N.A. T-6G), one for transport (Cessna U.17, Beaver, Cessna T-41, Otter, Twin Otter, Douglas C-47, PBY-5A) and one for helicopters (Bell H-13H)
TAM	Luque	Military Air Transport (Douglas C-47 & DC-3)
"Ará-Sunú" Aerobatic Team	Luque	North American T-6G Texan
GET	Luque	Tactical Training Group (Armed N.A. T-6D)
Paratrooper Regiment *"Silvio Pettirossi"*	Luque	Elite airborne infantry troops.

In 1980, through Law No. 832, the armed forces were reorganised in several commands.

Commander-in-Chief, exercised by the President of the Republic himself.

ARMY (*Ejército Paraguayo* – EP)
Table 4: Paraguayan Army Order of Battle, 1989

Unit	Base (or HQ)	Notes
Army Corps Command	Asunción	
Presidential Escort Regiment (REP)	Asunción	An infantry battalion, a military police battalion, small armoured element and field battery.
First Army Corps	Asunción	1st Infantry Division (with 14th Infantry Regiment *"Cerro Corá"* in Asuncion) 3rd Infantry Division (with 8th Infantry Regiment *"Piribebuy"* in San Juan Bautista) 1st Cavalry Division (with 1st Cavalry Regiment *"Valois Rivarola"*, 2nd Cavalry Regiment *'General Toledo"*, 3rd Cavalry Regiment *"Coronel Mongelos"* and 4th Cavalry Regiment *"Acá Carayá"*)

Second Army Corps	Villarrica	2nd Infantry Division (with the 27th Infantry Regiment "*General Garay*" in Villarrica) 4th Infantry Division (with the 5th Infantry Regiment "*General Diaz*" in Concepcion) 5th Infantry Division (with the 15th Infantry Regiment "*Lomas Valentinas*" in Pto. Pte. Stroessner).
Third Army Corps	Mcal. Estigarribia	6th Infantry Division (with the 6th Infantry Regiment "*Boquerón*" in Mcal. Estigarribia) 7th Infantry Division (with the 10th Infantry Regiment "*Sauce*" in Tte. Prat Gill) 8th Infantry Division (with the 4th Infantry Regiment "*Curupayty*" in Mayor Lagerenza).
Special Troops Command	Cerrito	A training School and one battalion.
Artillery Command	Paraguarí	1st Artillery Regiment "*Gral. Bruguez*" (including three artillery groups and an anti-aircraft artillery group, a training school and the 16th Infantry Regiment "*Mcal. Lopez*").
Engineering Corps Command	Asunción	A training School and five battalions.
Signal Corps Command	Asunción	A training School and one battalion.
Military Training School Command (CIMEE)	Asunción	The Military School "*Mariscal Francisco Solano Lopez*" in Capiatá, two Military Lyceums (one in Asunción and another in Encarnación), Officer School, NCO School, and School of Military Physical Education, all in Asunción.
Logistics Command	Asunción	10 General Directorates and a Military Hospital.

NAVY (*Armada de la República del Paraguay* – ARP)
Table 5: Paraguayan Navy Order of Battle, 1989

Unit	Base (or HQ)	Notes
Navy Command	Asunción	
War Fleet Command	Asunción	
Marine Infantry Command		Three bases, in Rosario (BIM 1), Vallemí (BIM 2) and Asunción (BIM 3)
Naval Aviation Command	Asunción	Helicopter Aero Naval Group (GAHE) in Asunción, General Purpose Aero Naval Group (GAPROGEN) and Training Aero Naval Group (GAEN), both at Asuncion International Airport in Luque.
Combat Support Command	Asunción	
Naval Training School Command (CINAE)	Asunción	
Coast Guard Command	Asunción	Five zones in the cities of Pilar, Alberdi, Asunción, Concepción and Olimpo, all ports on the Paraguay River. There were also Naval Detachments in Pto. Pte. Stroessner, Encarnación and Bahia Negra.
Naval Arsenal Command	Asunción	
Naval Logistics Command	Asunción	

From left to right: The Coat of Arms of the Paraguayan Army, Navy, Air Force and the Presidential Escort Regiment. (Author)

AIR FORCE (Fuerza Aérea Paraguaya – FAP)

The Paraguayan Air Arm went through a number of changes of name during its early history. When it was founded in 1923, the official name was the Military Aviation School; in 1932, at the outbreak of the Chaco War, it was known as Military Aviation in Campaign; after that war, it became the Paraguayan Air Arm; then once General Stroessner was president, The Aeronautics Command. Since the 1970s, the Military Aviation unofficially began to use the title Paraguayan Air Force. It was only some months after the 1989 *coup d'état* that the title Paraguayan Air Force (FAP) began to be used officially.

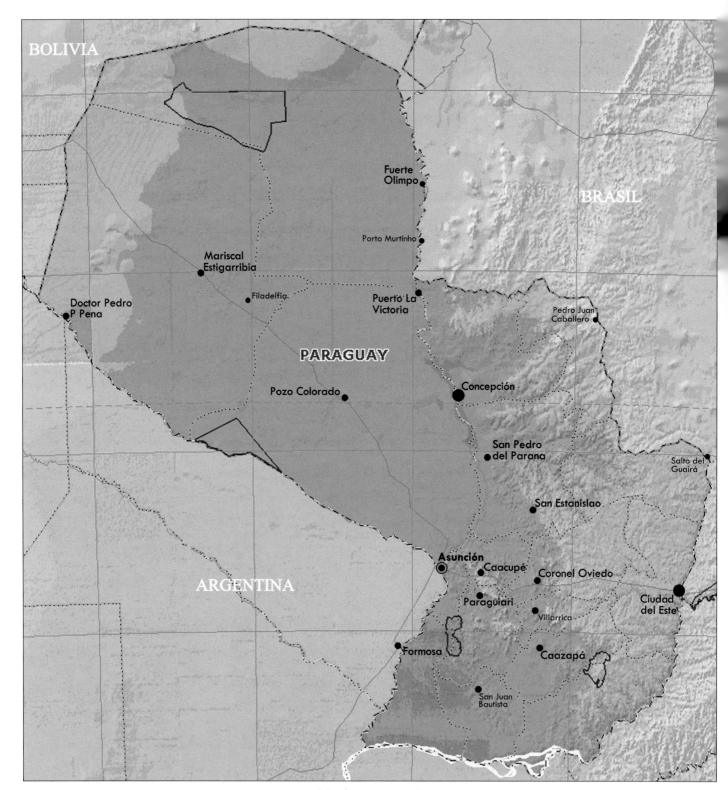
(Map by Tom Cooper)

Table 6: Paraguayan Air Force Order of Battle, 1989		
Unit	Base (or HQ)	Notes
Air Force Command	Ñu-Guazú, Luque	
1st Air Brigade	Silvio Pettirossi, Luque	Tactical Air Group (GAT), Training Air Group (GAE), Transport Air Group (GTA), Special Transport Air Group (GATE) and Helicopter Air Group (GAH).
Airborne Brigade	Ñu-Guazú, Luque	A Paratrooper Battalion, Logistics Battalion, Airborne Infantry Battalion, Security Battalion and Skydiving Squadron.
Air Logistics Command	Ñu-Guazú, Luque	Logistics, Ground Transport, War Material, Health Services, Air Supply Group (GAAB), Maintenance Air Group (GAM) and Air Force Recruiting Office.
Air Regions Command	Luque	Eastern and Western Regions Command, including four Air Bases in the Eastern Region and three in the Western Region. A Meteorology Section.
Air Force Training School Command (CIAERE)	Luque	Command and General Staff Course, different schools for Officers, NCOs, Air Force Reserve and languages.

2
PRELUDE TO THE COUP

Stroessner's decline

In 1987, Stroessner was 74 years old. He had already been in power for 33 years and was tired, with rapidly declining health and even rumours of cancer. His closest collaborators realised that "*Mi General*" would not live forever, and the few of them who dared to talk about the topic with him later revealed that he did not want to continue in the presidency of Paraguay. One of the possibilities was a campaign called "After Stroessner, another Stroessner", which was promoted by militant members of the Colorado Party. The "other" Stroessner was Alfredo's oldest son, Gustavo Stroessner Mora, who was an Air Force colonel, but was far less charismatic than his father. It seemed that General Stroessner disliked this idea, since he eventually agreed to be nominated as the presidential candidate of the Colorado Party for the 1988 elections, maybe for his last period, in order to gain time to find an acceptable successor.

By that time, there were two leading groups in the Colorado Party, the "traditionalists", whose members had been in the government for decades, and the "militants", the newer and more aggressive members. After a violent party convention on 1 August 1987, the militants definitively displaced the traditionalists, not only in key positions within the party, but also in government. The militant group fanaticism could have been perfectly compared with Hitler's *SchutzStaffel* (SS).

For decades, Stroessner had kept the military happy with high salaries, many extra benefits and, as mentioned before, unofficial permission to carry out all kinds of business. These key factors had ensured unquestioning loyalty to him in the armed forces. But with the arrival of the militant group in the Colorado Party and its incredible thirst for power and money, many things began to change. These changes upset many people, and a large group of Army officers, led by the by now Lieutenant General Andrés Rodriguez, tried to do something about it. Stroessner eased their fears by promising to keep control of the militants, but this only postponed the coup.

The discontent in the armed forces continued, with many high-ranking officers sent into retirement so that Colonel Gustavo Stroessner could be quickly promoted. At that time, there was one general of the Army – President Stroessner – 13 lieutenant generals – who had been in that rank for decades – 28 brigadier generals and almost 600 colonels. Fifty lieutenant colonels, Gustavo Stroessner among them, were promoted to colonel in December 1988. During January 1989, Stroessner decided to change some commanders, which proved very unfavourable for Lieutenant General Andrés Rodriguez.

On 20 January, Rodriguez himself, Vice Admiral Gonzalez Petit and Colonels Aníbal Regis Romero, Oscar Diaz Delmás, Orlando Machuca Vargas, Lorenzo Carrillo Melo and others, were sent into retirement; suspiciously, they were all the senior officers who had been conspiring against President Stroessner.

By the mid-1980s, Paraguay's economic boom generated in the previous decade with the construction of the Itaipú Dam had ended, as a consequence of which the Guaraní began to be devalued as the Central Bank issued an exaggerated amount of paper money to cover the fiscal deficits, causing inflation to soar. The situation worsened when the government decided to close all currency exchange houses, including the biggest one which belonged to Lieutenant General Andrés Rodriguez. When his business began to be affected, Rodriguez understood that he would be displaced from his position in the Army and decided to do something about it. Stroessner even told Rodriguez to accept the Ministry of Defence post or go into retirement, so as to remove him from his powerful position in the Army cavalry. This was the catalyst for the real beginning of the plot against Stroessner.

The Colorado Party's militant group, led by the infamous "Golden Four" (the private secretary of Stroessner, Mario Abdo Benitez, Minister of the Interior Sabino Augusto Montanaro, Minister of Health Dr Adan Godoy Gimenez and Minister of Labour and Justice Eugenio Jacquet), started being very verbally aggressive towards the American Ambassador in Paraguay, Clyde Taylor, who had criticised the government's violence against the people and opposition leaders, and the constant violation of human rights. This caused huge distress in bilateral relations, and all weapons and military training, along with intelligence reports from Washington, which had helped Stroessner, ceased. Meanwhile, the American Embassy moved closer to the Rodriguez group and eventually helped him with vital information for the crucial events to come. Due to the systematic violation of labour rights, the US Government also removed Paraguay from the Generalised System of Preferences (GSP), so no Paraguayan products would receive tax benefits in the American market.

Most people, even many of those ones who had supported the regime in the past, realised that Stroessner's time was up and that he would have to step aside for a new kind of government. There was general discontent, and although any dissent was brutally repressed, the size and number of protests increased alarmingly, supported by the opposition, which was organised under the *Acuerdo Nacional* (National Agreement) and the Catholic, German Evangelist and

An aged President Stroessner with the infamous "Golden Four" in 1987. (*ABC Color*)

Disciples of Christ Churches – under the name of the *Comité de Iglesias* (Churches Committee).

Pope John Paul II visited Paraguay in May 1988. His message gave hope to many people when he supported the work of the country's churches, saying: "The church cannot remain cornered in its temples."

On 15 August 1988, Stroessner started his eighth term in office, but was tired, senile and very weak, even becoming disconnected from reality. Instead of staying in office for five more years, he would remain in power for little more than five months. At the end of August, he had a prostate operation, and his recovery was long and painful. He could not stay more than two hours in his office in the government palace, and many of his orders were incoherent.

Meanwhile, the political situation continued to deteriorate, and by the end of the year, the Colorado Party militants had started a campaign to purge all officers of the Armed Forces opposed to Colonel Gustavo Stroessner succeeding his father as president.

Coup preparations

Even today, many people still think that General Andres Rodriguez was part of an altruistic military which brought democracy to Paraguay. The truth, however, is that Rodriguez led the coup against Stroessner because his economic interests were being affected. As mentioned above, he had been about to lead a coup just after the Colorado Party convention on 1 August 1987, and only stopped at the last minute after talking to the president. He was assured that the government was going to bring all the Colorado militants under control. Either Rodriguez naively believed this, or just decided to postpone the coup so that he could better prepare for it. Informally, directly after the party convention, a group of military officers and civilians started gathering in a so-called "Tennis Group" to discuss the political situation in Paraguay. The civilians included businessmen such as Guillermo Serrati, Enrique Diaz Benza, Desiderio Enciso, Francisco Appleyard and José Bogarín. The military, besides Rodriguez, included Brigadier Generals Eumelio Bernal and Víctor Aguilera Torres, Vice Admiral Eduardo González Petit and Colonels Pedro Ocampos, Oscar Díaz Delmás, Aníbal Regis Romero, Lino Cesar Oviedo, Hugo Escobar Anzoategui and Dionisio Cabello Amarilla. The meetings were held

Air Force Lt. Colonel Gustavo Stroessner Mora (centre) with his mother Ligia Mora (left) and wife Maria Eugenia "Pachi" Heikel (right). (Author)

for some time with great discretion so as not to raise suspicions in the government. Gustavo Stroessner was the first to learn about the conspiracy and warned his father about it, and that the leader of this group was his *protégé*, Lieutenant General Rodriguez. The dictator could not believe it and innocently disregarded all such reports. Even during the coup itself, Stroessner still did not believe that Rodriguez was behind it.

Although the US Government had previously had Rodriguez on its black list due to his alleged links with drug trafficking and other illegal businesses, it was understood that the commander of the powerful I Army Corps was the only one who could overthrow Stroessner. His "obscure past" was thus forgotten, and the American Embassy in Asunción soon started supporting Rodriguez.

Besides Rodriguez receiving the support of several military units, the Colorado traditionalists were also conspiring against the dictator. Among the civilian conspirators was Dr Luis Maria Argaña, ex-President of the Supreme Court of Justice, and Conrado Pappalardo Zaldivar, the head of the State Ceremonial Office, who was still

Two prominent civilian conspirators, Conrado "Teruco" Pappalardo Zaldivar (left) and Dr. Luis Maria "Lilo" Argaña (right). (*ABC Color*)

Left: Lt. Gen. Andrés Rodriguez Pedotti, Commander of the First Army Corps. (*Instituto de Historia y Museo Militar del MDN*). Right: Vice Admiral Eduardo González Petit, Commander of the Paraguayan Navy. (*Armada Paraguaya*)

working closely with Stroessner.

With the support of the US Government, Rodriguez then tried to convince most high-ranking officers of the armed forces to join the coup against Stroessner. Besides the obvious support of the entire 1st Cavalry Division, the infantry divisions and the Navy also joined the uprising. As for the Air Force, only its commander, Brigadier General Alcibiades Soto Valleau, and very few officers were loyal to Stroessner, while a great number of colonels and other ranks promised their support to Rodriguez. The Artillery Command was doubtful since it was Stroessner's historical arm, but the president would otherwise only have the support of the Presidential Escort Regiment and the police force.

During 1988, Rodriguez organised many secret meetings with high-ranking officers in the Army, Navy and Air Force, in order to plan the final attack. Rodriguez asked Colonel Santiago Zaracho, Operation Chief of the 1st Cavalry Division, to prepare an operational plan for the coup. This plan consisted mainly of four points: the isolation of the Presidential Escort Regiment; the occupation of the Ñu-Guazú Air Force Base; the seizure of the Police Headquarters; and the isolation of the Artillery in Paraguarí.

The ideal situation would have been to capture Stroessner and most key members of his regime without firing a single shot, and to avoid any loss of life. In the case of the dictator, the plan was to arrest him while he was on a private visit to his favourite mistress. However, if this plan failed, Rodriguez's troops would have to confront the Presidential Escort Regiment, the police force, the Air Force Paratrooper Regiment and the Artillery.

The coup would take place mainly in the capital, Asunción, and each force involved would prepare an operational plan. The Navy would attack the Police Headquarters, the Police Investigation Department and the Government Palace, and would block the Chacarita neighbourhood, where it was thought a paramilitary force of the militants could counterattack, and also seize the Channel 9 TV station. The 1st Infantry Division would neutralise the Army Signal Command, the Army Engineering Command and the Police Special Force Unit (FOPE). It would also take over the installations of the radio station *1o. de Marzo*, Channel 13 TV station, the national telephone company ANTELCO and some police stations. The Cavalry would neutralise the Presidential Escort Regiment. Rodriguez's plan for the Air Force was that officers loyal to him would remove vital parts from the Xavante and Tucano combat aircraft, and the Esquilo helicopters, so they could not be used against them, and also cooperate with the Navy in blocking of the Chacarita. Its troops would also block the access to the capital to prevent the arrival of the Artillery. The weakest element involved in the conspiracy, the Army Agropecuarial Battalion, would block traffic on Madame Lynch Avenue in order to secure one of the flanks of the Cavalry in their attack on the Presidential Escort Regiment.

"D-Day" was planned for Friday, 3 February 1989, a holiday; the festivity of St Blas, patron saint of Paraguay, and "H-Hour" was 3:00 a.m.

3

THE COUP

The Leader of the Coup: Lieutenant General Andrés Rodriguez Pedotti (1922–97)

Andrés Rodriguez was born on 15 June 1922 in the small town of Borja, Guairá, Paraguay. His parents were Marcos Rodriguez and Elisa Pedotti. He went to an elementary school in his hometown before his family moved to the capital, Asunción, where he went to high school. Since he was a child, he wanted to be a military man, and on 16 March 1942 he was accepted as a cadet in the Military School. There,

he chose to join the Cavalry, and once he graduated with the rank of sub-lieutenant in 1946, he was sent to the 2nd Cavalry Regiment "*Felipe Toledo*". During the revolution of 1947, he fought with the Government forces and was promoted to lieutenant in 1948, and then to 1st lieutenant the following year. It was then that he became a member of the Colorado Party.

During the presidency of Dr Federico Chaves, he was promoted to captain and was appointed as acting commander of the 3rd Cavalry

Lt. Gen. Andrés Rodriguez Pedotti, in combat uniform, the day of the Coup. (*El Diario Noticias*)

This young girl had two powerful grandfathers, Rodriguez and Stroessner. (Author)

Regiment "*Coronel Vicente Mongelós*". He married Nélida Reig Castellano in 1954 and later had three daughters, Dolly, Mirtha and Martha, the latter marrying Alfredo Stroessner Jr, known as Freddy.

In 1957, during the government of General Stroessner, he was promoted to major and was appointed as acting commander of the 1st Cavalry Division "*General Caballero*". He was promoted to lieutenant colonel in 1961, and the following year he became a teacher in the War School. In 1964, he was a full colonel and three years after that he was promoted to brigadier general and appointed as commander of the 1st Cavalry Division, a post that he would hold until 1981.

On 8 May 1969, he attended a demonstration of a Fairchild-Hiller PC-6 Turbo Porter at Asunción International Airport. He was invited to fly on the plane together with the commander of the Air Force, Brigadier General Adrian Jara, Dr Luis Migone and the pilot, Ernesto Vignoni. The PC-6 crashed into a parked Military Air Transport Convair CV-240 while taxiing, a fire broke out and the flames engulfed the plane. General Rodriguez managed to open one of the doors and escape from the doomed plane. He rolled on the ground to extinguish his burning clothes, which saved his life. Two of the other occupants, the pilot and the doctor, died, while General Jara was rescued by an Air Force sergeant, but died the following day due to his severe burns.

General Rodriguez later sued Fairchild-Hiller and eventually won his case in the US, receiving several million dollars in compensation for the accident. His family members have always justified the origins of his personal fortune from this award. However, according to many sources, including classified reports of the US government during the 1960s and 1970s, Rodriguez was linked to drug trafficking, mainly heroin and cocaine, together with other high-ranking military officers, although such charges were never formally proved. At the time, Rodriguez was seen as an enemy of the United States, and was one of Stroessner's *protégés*.

Rodriguez had other business interests, including *Cambios Guaraní*, the biggest exchange shop in Asunción, and had shares in an air taxi company called *Taxi Aéreo Guaraní S.A.* (TAGSA), an import-export business, and a copper wire company, among others. He also owned several ranches and became one of the richest men in Paraguay.

His final promotion during the Stroessner era was on 14 May 1970, becoming a lieutenant general. In 1981, under a restructuring of the Paraguayan armed forces, he was appointed as commander of the I Army Corps, the most powerful unit in the Paraguayan military.

By the late 1980s, once Rodriguez's businesses began to be affected and his powerful position in the Army was at stake, he started conspiring against the government, and on 2 February 1989, he led the *coup d'état* that overthrew Stroessner. He immediately assumed the provisional presidency and called for elections, in which several opposition parties participated. On 1 May 1989, he was declared the winner of the elections, with 72 percent of all the votes, and he served as president from 1988-93. At this time he was promoted to the highest rank in the military, General of the Army. During his government, a new constitution was prepared by the National Constituent Assembly, which did not include provision for re-election. Rodriguez was not pleased with this, but had to accept it. He supported the creation of the MERCOSUR – the South Common Market, a commercial alliance with Argentina, Brazil and Uruguay. After fresh elections in 1993, a new president came to power, the first civilian in more than 50 years, the engineer Juan Carlos Wasmosy Monti. Rodriguez subsequently refused to continue as political leader of the Colorado Party, despite the fact that he retired from power with a high popularity and acceptance rate. He died of liver cancer at the Methodist Hospital in

Dramatic picture sequence of the 1969 accident at Asunción International Airport. Gen. Rodriguez was the only survivor. (*ABC Color*)

New York on 21 April 1997.

The other military leaders

Even though almost all of the top-ranking officers were formed during the Stroessner's regime (1954-1989) and were very loyal to him for a long time, the deterioration of his government convinced

Table 7: The Carlos and Victor conspirators		
Rank and name	Position within the military	Code name
Lieutenant General Andrés Rodríguez Pedotti	I Army Corps Commander	CARLOS
Brigadier General Víctor Aguilera Torres	1st Cavalry Division Commander	CARLOS 1
Colonel Pedro de la Cruz C. Ocampos	2nd Cavalry Regiment Commander	CARLOS 2
Colonel Lino Cesar Oviedo Silva	3rd Cavalry Regiment Commander	CARLOS 3
Colonel Oscar Rodrigo Díaz Delmás	4th Cavalry Regiment Commander	CARLOS 4
Colonel Regis Aníbal Romero	Troop Division Commander	CARLOS 5
Brigadier General Eumelio Bernal	1st Infantry Division Commander	CARLOS 6
Vice Admiral Eduardo González Petit	Paraguayan Navy Commander	CARLOS 7
Colonel Francisco Luis Rodríguez	Army Cavalry	CARLOS 8
Colonel Lorenzo Carrillo Mello	1st Cavalry Regiment Commander	VICTOR 1
Colonel Dionisio Cabello Amarilla	Paraguayan Air Force	VICTOR 2
Colonel Jorge Mendoza Gaete	1st Cavalry Division Communication Chief	VICTOR 3
Colonel Luis Laguardia	I Army Corps Communication	VICTOR 4
Colonel Marino González	Frontier Battalion Commander	VICTOR 5

The 1989 Coup Commanders. (Author)

them that they should do something, but no one, except General Rodriguez, dared to even suggest a military action which was going to be considered high treason. They started to change their minds when Rodriguez convinced them that a change was possible.

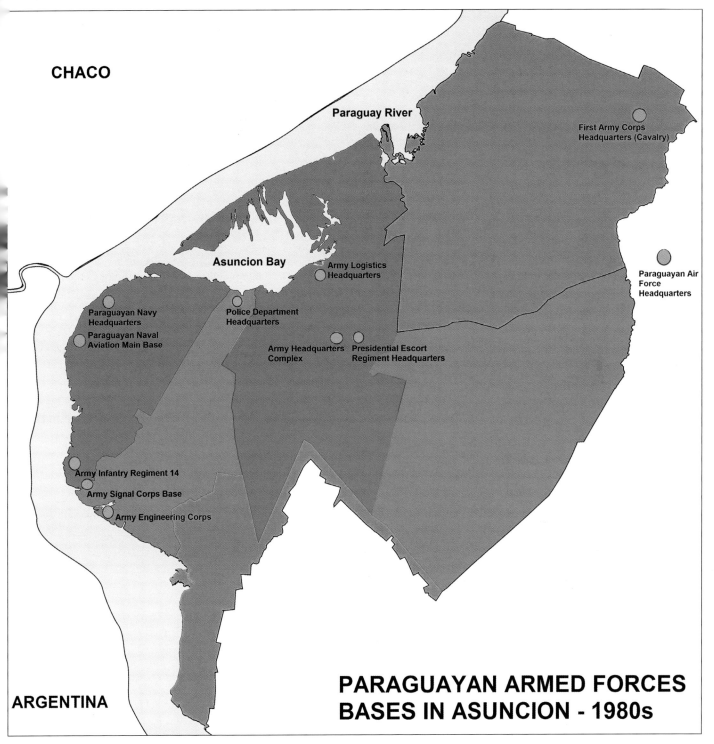

Paraguayan Armed Forces bases in Asunción. (Author)

Lt. Gen. Andres Rodriguez being sworn in as Paraguay's Constitutional President in 1989, immediately after the elections. (*ABC Color*)

Table 8: Paraguayan Army Armament, 1989	
Unit	Armament
Infantry	FN FAL and H&K G3A3 assault rifles, Browning M2, FN MAG and H&K 21E machine guns. Standard combat uniform of dark olive green fatigues and American M1 helmet. Troop transports: Toyota FA/DA 100 and Chevrolet trucks, and jeeps.
Cavalry	15 M3A1 Stuart light tanks with a 37mm M6 gun. 28 Engesa EE-9 Cascavel multirole armoured vehicles with an Engesa EC-90 90mm gun and a coaxial 7.62mm MG. 12 Engesa EE-11 Urutú armoured personnel carriers, with a single turret with a 7.62mm MG. Its troops used either FN FAL or H&K G3A3 assault rifles, as well as Browning M2, FN MAG and H&K 21 MGs. Troop transports: Unimog trucks and jeeps.
Artillery	18 105mm M101 howitzers. 12 88mm British Ordnance QF-25/South African Q-1 howitzers. 12 75mm Bofors cannons and 12 75mm Krupp cannons. 20 20mm Oerlikon Type S A-A cannons and 3 20mm Oerlikon GA-BO1 A-A cannons. 118 81mm Brandt mortars, 8 107mm M32 mortars and 42 60mm Spanish-made mortars. Also, bazookas and light anti-tank weapons, including 6 106mm CSR M40A1s, 31 75mm FSR M20s, 32 57mm M18s and 136 portable M-20s.
Others	Agropecuarian Service, Logistics Service, Health Service, Engineering Corps and Signal Corps, all of them with light armament including pistols, assault rifles and machine guns, and a variety of trucks and jeeps.

Table 9: Paraguayan Navy Armament, 1989	
Unit	Armament
War Fleet	Twin gunboats C.1 *Paraguay* and C.2 *Humaitá* each with four 120mm, three 76mm guns and two 40mm and two 20mm cannons. They were inoperative.
	Gunboat P-01 *Capitan Cabral*, with a single 40mm Bofors cannon, two 20mm Oerlikon AA cannons and two 12.7mm MGs.
	Gunboats P-02 *Nanawa* and P-04 *Tte. Fariña*, with four double 40mm Bofors cannons and two 12.7mm MGs.
	Gunboat P-05 (P.2) *Itaipú*, with a single 40mm Bofors cannon, two 81mm mortars and four 12.7mm MGs and a helicopter platform.
	Command Boat BC-1 *Boquerón*, with a helicopter platform and some defensive 12.7mm MGs but inoperative.
	Eight 701 Class patrol boats, with 12.7mm MGs.
	Four unarmed tugs.
	Three LCVPs
	Transport Boat *Tte. Herreros* and Freighter *Guaraní*.
	A presidential yacht.
Marine Infantry Corps	Elite unit armed with light weapons, mortars, bazookas and howitzers.
Naval Aviation	Two Helibras HB-350 Esquilo which were armed wtih twin MG or rocket launchers pods.
	Two Bell H-13H patrol helicopters.
	Two Hiller UH-12E patrol helicopters.
	One Cessna U206C and a Cessna 310 transports and a pair of Cessna 150 trainers.

Paraguayan Army Infantry Regiment 14 officers with a Toyota Jeep during a parade in the 1980s (Carlos Corvalán)

Infantry troops during a parade in 1970. (*ABC Color*)

Infantry troops with a mortar during military manoeuvres in the 1980s. (Col. Luis Vittone)

The Military Uprising

In mid-January 1989, the Cavalry troops began a series of shooting exercises. Brigadier General Victor Aguilera Torres, the commander of the 1st Cavalry Division, ordered the withdrawal of a series of arms from the Army arsenal, including machine guns, bazookas and hand grenades, as well as ammunition. Radio equipment was also installed in several jeeps and vehicles used by the division and regiment commanders. For better communication, a radio antenna was moved from the Piribebuy area, 80km away from Asunción, to Fernando de la Mora, just a few kilometres from the capital.

As regards the Navy, the Marines also started a series of combat exercises in the final months of 1988 at the Sajonia Naval Base in Asunción. The Naval Aviation's Esquilo helicopters offered

Cavalry Engesa EE-9 Cascavel multirole armoured vehicles. (Renato Angulo)

Cavalry Engesa EE-11 Urutú armoured personnel carriers. (Carlos Corvalan)

An M3A1 Stuart light tank. (Author)

Table 10: Paraguayan Air Force Armament, 1989	
Unit	Armament
GAT	7 Embraer EMB-326/AT-26 Xavante with two 12.7mm Browning MGs in under wing pods and four hard points with a max. Load of 1,841 kg including bombs and 70mm rocket launchers.
	6 Embraer EMB-312/AT-27 Tucano, with four hard points for a max. Load of 1,000 kg, including 7.62mm Twin MAG Pod FN Herstal MGs, Mk.81/82 bombs or Avibras M2A1 180Kg napalm bombs, and Avibras 70/7M5A or Equipaer EQ-LMF-70/7AP rocket launchers with seven tubes.
GAE	6 North American T-6D with one fixed and one movable 7.62mm MGs and four under wing hard points to carry bombs or rocket launchers.
	15 unarmed North American T-6G advanced trainers.
	4 Neiva T-25 Universal basic trainers.
	6 Aerotec T-23 Uirapurú primary trainers.
GTA (TAM)	6 Douglas C-47
	4 CASA C.212-200 Aviocar
	1 Convair C-131D Samaritan
	1 Consolidated-Vultee PBY-5A Catalina
	1 De Havilland DHC-6-200 Twin Otter (Presidential plane)
GATE	2 Cessna U.17
	4 Cessna U206G
	1 Cessna 337
	2 Cessna T-41B
	2 Cessna 402
	1 De Havilland DHC-2 Beaver
GAH	4 Helibras HB-350 Esquilos, armed with MG or rocket launcher pods.
	2 Bell UH-1B
	1 Hiller SL4
	1 Hiller SL4T

Table 11: Presidential Escort Regiment Armament, 1989	
Unit	Armament
REP	Well-equipped troops with assault rifles, machine guns and pistols
	Bazookas and mortars.
	3 Sherman Firefly "Repotenciado" tanks re-armed with a French 105mm gun.
	3 Chrysler M2 Half Track armoured vehicles with 20mm AA guns
	4 M101 105mm howitzers.
	A number of Toyota FA/DA 100 trucks for troop transports.

Table 12: Police Department Armament, 1989	
Unit	Armament
Regular police force	Light arms, mainly pistols, revolvers and submachine guns. Patrol cars and transport trucks.
Special Police Operation Force (FOPE)	Elite force with assault rifles, submachine guns and MGs. Transport trucks. The local SWAT.
Fire Brigade	
Motorized Unit	With motorcycles.

demonstration of their firepower in December at an event that was attended by General Rodriguez.

Stroessner and Rodriguez met for the last time on 20 January in an informal meeting of senior officers at the Hotel-Casino Itá Enramada. Since Rodriguez thought that he was going to be captured that day, he discretely went with several armed guards and had an Esquilo helicopter and a pilot, Captain PAM (*Piloto Aviador Militar*/Military Aviator Pilot) Victor Insfrán, at Ñu-Guazú AFB ready to pick him up, but nothing happened. There was another meeting, this time a more formal one, in the Armed Forces Headquarters complex on 26 January, an ideal occasion for the president's arrest, so Rodriguez planned a ruse not to go, stating that he had fallen and broken a leg, which was in a cast.

On the morning of 2 February, the graduation ceremony of Army Reserve officers took place at the Campo Grande Cavalry base, with the most important civilian and military authorities of the government,

The Army Artillery Headquarters in the city of Paraguarí. (*Comando de Artilleria del Ejercito*)

88mm British Ordnance QF-25/ South African Q-1 howitzers. (*Comando de Artilleria del Ejército*)

A pair of 75mm Bofors cannons. (*Comando de Artillería del Ejercito*)

THE 1989 COUP D'ETAT IN PARAGUAY: THE END OF A LONG DICTATORSHIP, 1954–1989

Paraguayan Cavalry M3A1 Stuart light tank with a 37mm M6 gun. The U.S. donated nine Stuart M3A1 in 1969 and Brazil subsequently donated twelve M3 & M3A1. In the 1980s, most of them were re-equipped with a Scania Vabis D11 diesel engine in Brazil. Incredibly, some are still active at the time of writing. They belonged to the 3rd Cavalry Regiment 3 (RC3). (Artwork by David Bocquelet)

Paraguayan Presidential Escort Regiment (REP) M4A3 Sherman Firefly V tank with the initial colour scheme of overall satin olive drab. Three Fireflies, each armed with a British 17-Pdr gun, were donated by the Argentinean Army in 1971, and another three in 1981. They were powered by a 10-litre Continental V12 engine. They remained in service until the late 1980s when three of them were exchanged for three Sherman "Repotenciado" from Argentina in 1988. (Artwork by David Bocquelet)

Paraguayan Presidential Escort Regiment (REP) modified M4A3 Sherman "Repotenciado" tank with a L44/47 FTR 105mm main gun. Three examples were received by the REP in exchange of the Fireflies V from Argentina in the late 1980s. They were powered by a Poyaud 520 V8 Diesel engine and received a tactical camouflage of dark green and tan. These were the ones which were active during the 1989 coup and remained on strength in the REP until 2018 when they were finally withdrawn from service. (Artwork by David Bocquelet)

During the 1980s, Brazil donated a total of 12 Chrysler M2 halftracks to the Paraguayan Presidential Escort Regiment (REP), and these were armed with 20mm anti-aircraft guns. Some were subsequently used by the Cavalry, while three remained with the REP by the time of the coup of 1989. As usual, their camouflage pattern consisted of dark green and tan. (Artwork by David Bocquelet)

Paraguayan Cavalry Engesa EE-9 Cascavel multirole armoured vehicle with an Engesa EC-90 90mm gun and a coaxial 7.62mm MG. 28 Cascavel vehicles were purchased new from Brazil in the late 1980s for the Cavalry and they were all active in the 1989 coup. As obvious from the crest applied on its turret, this vehicle belonged to the 2nd Cavalry Regiment (RC.2). (Artwork by David Bocquelet)

Paraguayan Cavalry Engesa EE-11 Urutú armoured personnel carrier, with a Cadillac turret including a 7.62mm MG. Paraguay acquired a total of 12 Urutús from Brazil in the late 1980s for the 2nd Cavalry Regiment and all were deployed during the 1989 coup. As in the case of the Cascavels, the camouflage pattern consisted of dark green and tan. (Artwork by David Bocquelet)

THE 1989 COUP D'ETAT IN PARAGUAY: THE END OF A LONG DICTATORSHIP, 1954–1989

A North American T-6G Texan of the Training Air Group (GAE), Paraguayan Air Force, based at Ñu-Guazú AFB in Luque. Brazil donated 15 T-6Gs in the 1970s and South Africa another 15 in 1979-80. The sample illustrated had the South African Air Force (SAAF) color scheme in dayglo orange, gray and bare metal. At the time of the Coup, only 12 of them were operational. They were withdrawn from use in 1991. (Artwork by Tom Cooper)

A North American T-6D Texan of the Training Air Group (GAE), Paraguayan Air Force, based at Ñu-Guazú AFB in Luque. The T-6Ds were armed with one fixed and one movable 7.62mm MG and four under wing hard points to carry bombs or rocket launchers. Brazil donated 15 T-6Ds in the 1970s and they all received a disruptive camouflage pattern consisting in dark green and light gray on top surfaces, and bare metal on the bottom. At the time of the 1989 Coup, only six were still on strength but they were wfu at the end of that year. (Artwork by Tom Cooper)

A Cessna T-41B Mescalero of the Special Transport Air Group (GATE), based at Ñu-Guazú AFB in Luque. Five T-41Bs were donated by the Military Assistance Program (MAP) of the American Government in 1974. Two of them were in service in 1989 and both were painted in a camouflage in the same light gray and dark green as in the UH-1Bs and T-6Ds, plus some dayglo orange in the nose, tail and wing tips. The bottom surfaces were painted in dark olive drab. (Artwork by Tom Cooper)

(iii)

A Bell UH-1B of the Helicopter Air Group (GAH), Paraguayan Air Force, based at Ñu-Guazú AFB in Luque. The FAP purchased two second-hand UH-1Bs in the USA in 1982 and both of them were on strength in 1989. Camouflage pattern consisted of the same colours as applied on the T-6Gs, including light grey and dark green. Markings included the fin flash, the service title and a small serial applied on the fin (the latter was repeated in white on the forward fuselage). (Artwork by Tom Cooper)

In 1987, Paraguay acquired four Helibras HB.350 Esquilos – a version of the well-known Eurocopter AS.350B2/B3 Écureuil helicopter, designed in France but produced in Brazil under licence. All four were assigned to the Helicopter Air Group (GAH), based at Ñu-Guazú AFB in Luque. Three were still on strength in 1989: with the help of a pylon installed through the rear cabin, they could be armed with Equipaer EQ-LMF-70/7AP pods for unguided 68mm rockets (shown here) and FN ETNA TMP-5 twin 7.62mm machine gun pods. (Artwork by Tom Cooper)

The Helicopter Aero Naval Group (GAHE) of the Paraguayan Naval Aviation was bolstered through the acquisition of two Helibras HB.350 Esquilos in 1985. Contrary to the examples operated by the air force, they wore this relatively simple livery consisting of ghost grey overall, with the entire fin in national colours. Based at the Naval Air Station Sajonia, in Asunción, both examples took part in the 1989 coup, when they were armed with FN ETNA TMP-5 7.62mm machine gun pods. (Artwork by Tom Cooper)

THE 1989 COUP D'ETAT IN PARAGUAY: THE END OF A LONG DICTATORSHIP, 1954–1989

This Embraer EMB.326GB (i.e. AT-26 Xavante) of the First Fighter Squadron of the Tactical Air Group (GAT), Paraguayan Air Force, based at Asunción International Airport in Luque, is known to have been actively involved in the coup of 1989. The Xavantes were usually armed with two 12.7mm Browning MGs in under wing pods, but could carry additional ordnance – including light bombs and pods for unguided rockets - on four underwing hardpoints. Out of ten examples purchased from Brazil in 1979-1980, seven were still operational at the time of the coup. (Artwork by Tom Cooper)

Embraer EMB.312 (AT-27 Tucano) of the Special Air Operations Squadron of the Tactical Air Group (GAT), Paraguayan Air Force, based at Asunción International Airport in Luque. Paraguay acquired six newly-built aircraft from Brazil in 1987 and all were operational as of 1989. They had four underwing hardpoints, and could be armed with FN ETNA twin 7.62mm machine gun pods (manufactured by FN Hersal), Mk.81 and Mk.82 bombs, Equipaer EQ- LMF-70/7AP rocket launchers and 180kg Avibras M2A1 napalm bombs. (Artwork by Tom Cooper)

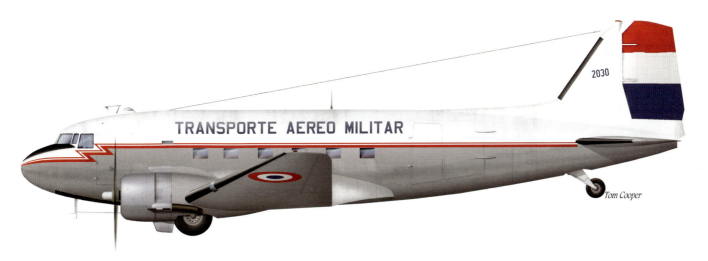

A Douglas C-47A-10-DK of the Military Air Transport (TAM), Transport Air Group (GTA), *Fuerza Aerea Paraguaya*. A total of 5 Douglas DC-3 and 27 Douglas C-47 saw service in TAM between 1953 and 2003. Five were purchased in the U.S. in the 1950s, 20 were donated through MAP between 1962 and 1973, 3 by Argentina in 1969, 2 by Chile in 1981 and 2 by Brazil in 1984. All of them were intensively used in scheduled flights between 1953 and 1998. (Artwork by Tom Cooper)

(v)

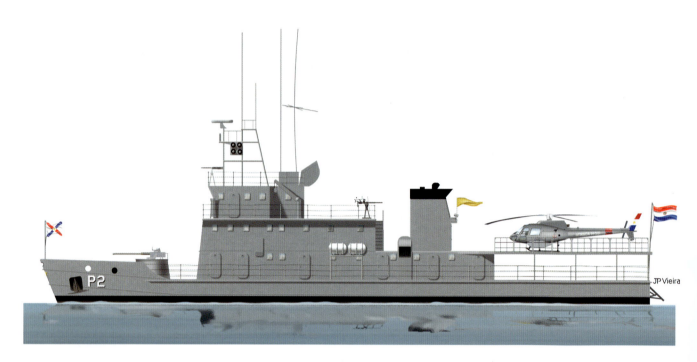

Paraguayan Navy gunboat P.2 (later re-numbered P-05) *Itaipú*, armed with a single 40mm Bofors cannon, two 81mm mortars and four 12.7mm MGs, with a rear helicopter platform, and based at Sajonia Naval Base in Asunción. An example of the Brazilian *Roraima* Class, it was purchased new from Brazil in 1985 and it is still in service in the Navy at the time of writing. The displacement is 365 tons at full load; it is powered by 2 MAN V6V16 / 18TL diesel engines of 1,920 hp. It has a maximum speed of 14 knots and a range of 6,000 nautical miles at 12 knots. It carries 9 officers and 31 crew members. (Artwork by J P Vieira)

Paraguayan Navy gunboat P-01 *Capitán Cabral*, armed with a single 40mm Bofors cannon, two 20mm Oerlikon AA cannons and two 12.7mm MGs. Based at Sajonia Naval Base in Asunción, it was built in the Netherlands in 1907 and purchased by Paraguay in 1908. It participated in the Revolutions of 1922 and 1947, and the Chaco War. In 1980, it was completely refurbished in the Navy Arsenal, where it was re-engined with a 360hp diesel Caterpillar 3408. It has a maximum speed of 9 knots, with its crew of 25 and displacement at full load of 206 tons. It is still in the Navy's service at the time of writing. (Artwork by J P Vieira)

THE 1989 COUP D'ETAT IN PARAGUAY: THE END OF A LONG DICTATORSHIP, 1954–1989

A pair of FAP EMB.312/AT-27 Tucanos in flight. (Michel Anciaux)

A HB.350 Esquilo of the FAP (Author)

A DC-6B of the TAM. (Alberto Fortner)

(vii)

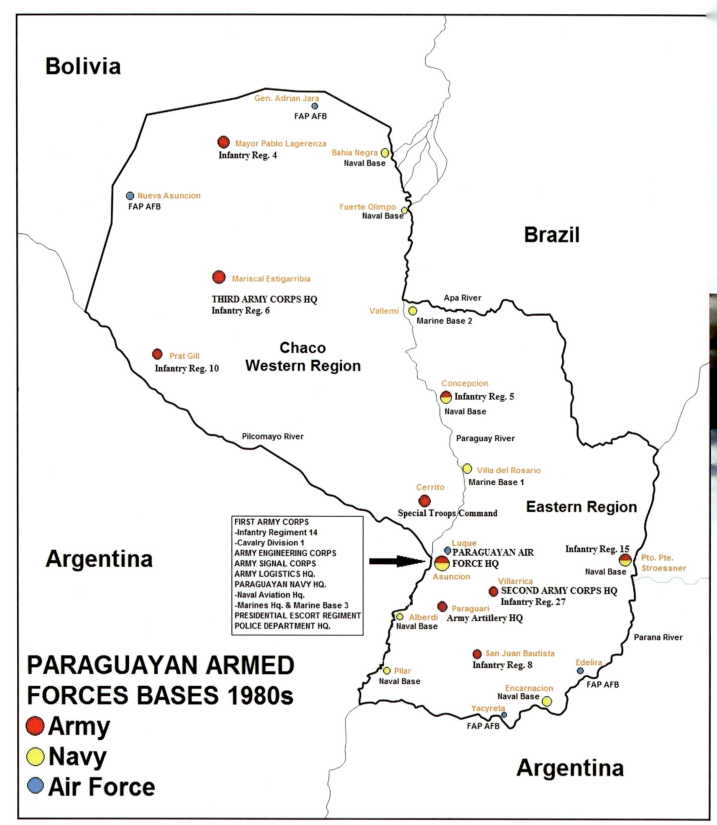
Paraguayan Armed Forces' bases in the 1980s. (Author)

A 40mm L/60 Bofors Anti-Aircraft canon. (*Comando de Artillería del Ejercito*)

From left to right, the Coat of Arms of various Army units, the Engineering Corps, the Signal Corps, the Agropecuarian Service, the Logistics Service and the Health Service. (Paraguayan Army)

Paraguayan Navy patrol boat P-01 *Capitán Cabral*. (*Armada Paraguaya*)

The Paraguayan Navy Anchor and Yellow Star. (*Armada Paraguaya*)

Gunboat C.1 *Paraguay*. (*Armada Paraguaya*)

The Command Boat B.C.1 *Boquerón*. (*Armada Paraguaya*)

Gunboat P.2 (later P-05) *Itaipú* with a Naval Aviation *Esquilo* helicopter. (*Armada Paraguaya*)

A Paraguayan Navy Marine platoon with mortars. (*Armada Paraguaya*)

Paraguayan Naval Aviation (ANP) Helibras HB-350 Esquilo. (*Aviación Naval Paraguaya*)

ANP Bell H-13Hs at Sajonia NAS in the 1970s. (*Aviación Naval Paraguaya*)

ANP Hiller UH-12Es at Sajonia NAS in the 1980s. (*Aviación Naval Paraguaya*)

ANP Cessna 150M at Asuncion International Airport in the late 1980s. (Author)

ANP Cessna 310K at Asunción International Airport in the late 1980s. (Author)

ANP Cessna U206C. (Author)

Paraguayan Naval Aviation emblem. (Author)

who did not notice anything unusual there. Rodriguez was not present due to his "broken leg", and once the ceremony was over, some officials visited him in his house and could see that he had a cast on one leg.

Meanwhile, all the final details were being readied for the coup. Radio communication was vital for the success of the putsch, so all orders were transmitted personally by Rodriguez to all the other key conspirators, who were given the code names "Carlos" or "Victor". Radio equipment was installed not only in the Cavalry Headquarters but also in many vehicles, mainly jeeps. All Cavalry troops and officers were in combat uniform in the afternoon, and at 7:00 p.m. had a special dinner. The code name for the uprising was "Operation 33" – for 3 February at 3:00 a.m. – but last-minute changes had to be made because news of the proposed coup leaked out. Rodriguez was informed that Stroessner was going to visit his mistress, and ordered his capture there. Stroessner was a man of habits, and that evening he had already planned to play cards with Colonel Feliciano Duarte, the president of the national telephone company, ANTELCO. When visiting his friends and his mistresses, he used to take a bodyguard of 18 members of the Presidential Escort Regiment. At 5:00 p.m. that day, Stroessner arrived at Colonel Duarte's house and started playing cards. He was interrupted by a call from his son, Gustavo, who told him the coup would take place that day. Stroessner told him that was nonsense and hung up to continue playing cards. At 7:00 p.m., Stroessner and his escort went to the house of Estela "Ñata" Legal, his favourite mistress, with whom he had two daughters. He had not been there for several months due to his delicate health – he had not recovered well from the prostate surgery in August 1988. Two military spies who were close to the house radioed a warning message to the Cavalry Headquarters, "The duck is in the nest", and so the operation was launched.

The official watchword for troops loyal to Rodriguez was set to "Puente Remanso", a bridge connecting the two main regions of Paraguay, near Asunción. A commando force of the 4th Cavalry Regiment "*Acá-Carayá*" composed of 40 well-trained and well-armed soldiers, NCOs and officers in trucks, led by Colonels Mauricio Díaz Delmás and Eduardo Allende, was entrusted with the arrest of the dictator at his mistress' home. The mission was organised by Colonels Marino González and Regis Aníbal Romero. The trucks belonged

FAP Embraer EMB-326GB/AT-26 Xavante. (FAP)

FAP N.A. T-6D Texan. (via João Carlos Zeitoun Moralez)

to the Army Agropecuarian Service, one to transport cattle and the other grains, so as not to attract the attention of loyal supporters of the regime. 1st Lieutenant Melgarejo and Lieutenant Benitez would assault the house with two combat groups to capture Stroessner, while the left flank would be taken care of by a combat group led by Lieutenant Colonel Cano and the right flank by another group under Captain Ramirez. Other combat groups led by Colonel Allende and Lieutenant Patiño would arrest the Escort Regiment bodyguards. Stroessner was already aware of the plot, and at 8:30 p.m. hurriedly escaped to his second son's house, leaving half of the escort personnel at Legal's house. One of the trucks hit a metal fence and a brisk firefight developed between the Escort Regiment and Colonel Diaz Delmás' troops, the latter of which suffered eight fatalities and several wounded officers. Although the operation was a failure, the attacking force eventually seized the house. Estela Legal and her family members were later captured and taken away. Since Stroessner was not captured, the leaders of the uprising had to anticipate the actions of the military still loyal to him.

General Francisco Ruiz Diaz, the commander of the Presidential Escort Regiment, immediately learned about the situation and quickly went to his unit to get it ready for action to defend the regime.

Stroessner arrived at the house of his son, Freddy, by 9:00 p.m. and was joined by his other son, Gustavo, daughter Graciela and another 50 members of the Presidential Escort Regiment. The building was not deemed to be safe, so they all moved to the Presidential Escort Regiment barracks, not far from there. Upon arrival, it was suggested to Stroessner to move again to the adjacent Armed Forces Headquarters complex where the concrete building had a heliport that could have been used to evacuate the president in case of an attack. Once there, the president and his family were joined by other loyalists, including Minister of Defence Lieutenant General Germán Martínez, Army Chief of Staff Lieutenant General Alejandro Fretes Dávalos, Military Training School commander Lieutenant General Gerardo Johannsen Roux, Presidential Escort Regiment commander Brigadier General Francisco Ruiz Diaz, Chief of Military Intelligence Brigadier General Benito Guanes Serrano and two other generals, Bernardino Peralta Baez and César Machuca Vargas. There were also Colonels Pedro Hugo Cañete, Benito Pereira, Ramón Martínez, Carlos Maggi and Catalino González Rojas, Major Orlando Oviedo, Lieutenant Lefevre, eight soldiers and government notary Juan José Benitez Rickmann.

Lieutenant General Rodriguez met Colonel Lino Oviedo at the 3rd Cavalry Regiment base to coordinate the attack on the Armed Forces

Presidential Escort Regiment (REP) Sherman Firefly tanks. (*Instituto de Historia y Museo Militar del MDN*)

REP M2 Half Track armoured vehicle. (*Instituto de Historia y Museo Militar del MDN*)

REP troops. (Author)

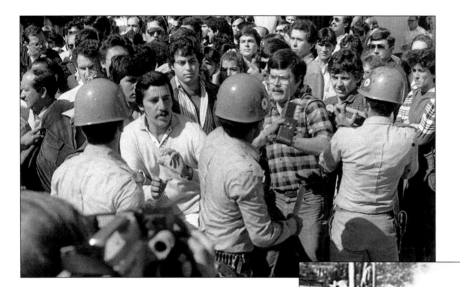

Police officers blocking a university students' gathering in downtown Asunción in the late 1980s. (*ABC Color* & *Ultima Hora*)

The Police force using tear gas against members of the opposition during a march in Asunción in the late 1980s. (*ABC Color* & *Ultima Hora*)

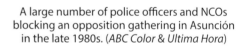

A large number of police officers and NCOs blocking an opposition gathering in Asunción in the late 1980s. (*ABC Color* & *Ultima Hora*)

Two opposition leaders, Domingo Laino (second from the right) of the Liberal Party, and Luis Resck (with glasses in the centre) of the Christian Democratic Party, being arrested by the police during a violent march in Asunción in the late 1980s. (*ABC Color* & *Ultima Hora*)

María Estela *"Ñata"* Legal's house (left). Stroessner's "other" family, with his favorite mistress *"Ñata"* Legal. (Dr. Hermes Gomez Ginard)

The Presidential Escort Regiment main building (left) and the Army Headquarters Complex (right), Stroessner's bunker during the coup. (Author)

Headquarters complex, which had originally been set for 3:00 a.m., but due to recent events had to be carried out immediately. Colonel Oviedo ordered the general mobilisation of all troops, and at 9:15 p.m. they all headed to Stroessner's bunker with 14 Stuart light tanks and 120 men carried in a convoy of jeeps and Unimog trucks. At the same time, wheeled armoured vehicles and troops led by Colonel Regis Romero headed for the Paraguayan Air Force main base at Ñu-Guazú. Just a month before, Stroessner had changed the FAP commander; Lieutenant General Luis González Ravetti, who had been in the post since 1977 and went into retirement, to be replaced by Brigadier General Alcibiades Ramón Soto Valleau, who was very loyal to the dictator.

Colonel Oviedo's forces were deployed opposite the Army School of Physical Education on Gral. Santos Avenue and facing the barracks of the Presidential Escort Regiment on Mariscal Lopez Avenue. Some troops and armoured vehicles were also sent to the rear of the Armed Forces Headquarters complex so as to completely encircle it.

The commander of the 2nd Cavalry Regiment, Colonel Pedro Ocampos, received a radio message from Lieutenant General Rodriguez about the course of events, so he immediately drove from Cerrito (in Chaco) to his unit in Asunción. He sent five EE-9 Cascavel armoured vehicles to support Colonel Regis Romero's troops in neutralising the Air Force, another pair of them to support the Navy deployment in the Government Palace and 12 more to face the Presidential Escort Regiment.

A third group, 90-strong, from the 1st Cavalry Regiment, led by Colonel Lorenzo Carrillo Melo, equipped with four 81mm and two 60mm mortars, positioned themselves on the terrace of the Army Physical Education School, aiming at the Presidential Escort Regiment area. They also had assault rifles, machine guns, a rocket launcher and two Toyota pick-up trucks, each with a .50 calibre machine gun.

All the above-mentioned groups opened fire on the Presidential Escort Regiment and the Armed Forces Headquarters complex, causing heavy damage. The resistance of troops loyal to Stroessner was limited, mainly because in the previous days, many officers, NCOs and soldiers were sent on vacation, and infiltrated agents had unloaded most of the arms available to those that remained. A recent Taiwanese donation of arms was still in its wooden crates and could not be used in the defence of the base. The Sherman tanks could not move due to the lack of personnel to operate them, and even if they could get someone to do it, they lacked fuel. One M2 Half Track dared to go out of the base to try to repel the attack, but it was immediately hit by a shell from a Stuart tank and neutralised.

A 37mm shell from one of the Colonel Oviedo's Stuart tanks knocked down a huge tree that cut the main electricity lines in the area, while a sniper, William Wilka, on a FAP Esquilo helicopter crewed by Captain PAM Victor Insfrán hit and destroyed the emergency power generator of the Presidential Escort Regiment.

On the day of the attack, most of the personnel of the Presidential Escort Regiment were untrained privates, with very few officers and

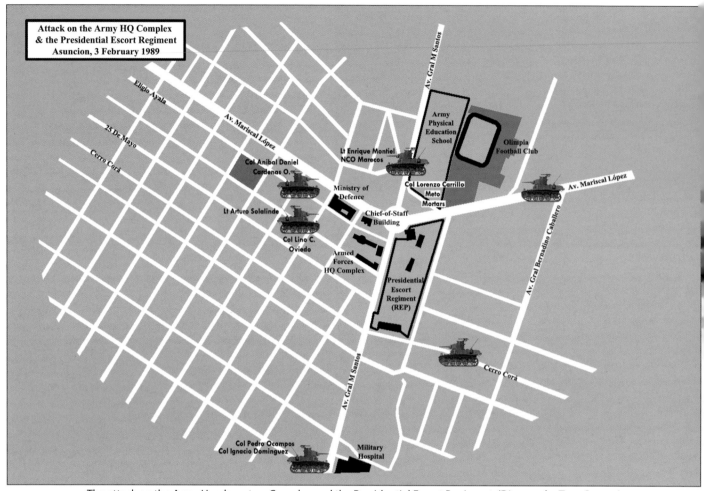

The attack on the Army Headquarters Complex and the Presidential Escort Regiment. (Diagram by Tom Cooper)

Cavalry Stuart light tanks. (*Instituto de Historia y Museo Militar del MDN*)

NCOs, so the number of fatalities was very high. The official list prepared by the new government set the number at 36, but there were actually 137 fatalities in the area, including an officer loyal to Rodriguez, Major Miguel Angel Ramos Alfaro, who was seriously injured by a grenade splinter and died on the way to the hospital. Many of the Escort Regiment's soldiers were also wounded.

The besieged troops loyal to Stroessner now made frantic calls for all possible military and police units to support them with a counterattack. They could only reach the Police Headquarters, but they were being attacked by Navy forces. Colonel Gustavo Stroessner called the Air Force base several times to order combat planes to strike the conspirators, talking to Colonels Enrique Yebrán, Miguel Angel Segovia and Alberto Chiola, who tried to organise resistance, but the cavalry troops of Colonel Regis Romero had already taken the base by assault, arresting the FAP commander, Brigadier General Alcibiades Soto, and all the officers loyal to the regime. Other cavalry troops, in connivance with FAP officers, arrested the Tactical Air Group commander, Colonel Marino Ruiz Alonso.

President Stroessner, who was able to listen to the conspirators' radio communications because he had very powerful radio equipment in his bunker, was finally convinced that Lieutenant General Rodriguez was behind the coup. He first thought that the uprising was led by a group of colonels and that Rodriguez was also a victim, but the messages he heard finally convinced him otherwise. At 12:35 a.m.,

Left: A Paraguayan Air Force armed Helibras HB-350 Esquilo. (FAP) Right: Captain PAM Victor *"Chino"* Edgar Insfrán Diana. (Col. Carlos Melgarejo)

Presidential Escort Regiment (REP) Sherman Firefly tanks. (Carlos Corvalan)

A REP M2 Half Track vehicle during a parade in the 1980s. (Carlos Corvalán)

Troops of the Infantry Regiment 14. (Author)

after an infantry platoon led by Major Virgilio Cano seized the *1ro. de Marzo* radio station, an official declaration recorded by Lieutenant General Rodriguez was aired:

> Dear compatriots, dear members of the Armed Forces. We have left our barracks in defence of the dignity and honour of the Armed Forces; for the full and total unification of the Colorado Party in the government; for the initiation of democratisation in Paraguay; for the respect of Human Rights; for the defence of our Christian religion, Roman Apostolic Catholic. That is what I am offering you with the sacrifice of the Paraguayan soldier to our dear, brave and noble Paraguayan people. I hope that the comrades of the Armed Forces accompany me in these circumstances, because we are defending a noble and just cause.

Immediately after Rodriguez's announcement, other important military units in the interior of the country, such as the 4th Infantry Division in Concepción, under Brigadier General Humberto Garcete, rose in support of the conspirators. Similar actions were taken by the 3rd Infantry Division, in San Juan Bautista, with its commander Brigadier General Juan de Dios Garbett, the 8th Infantry Division in Lagerenza, Chaco, led by Brigadier General Ismael Otazú, and Brigadier General Ramón Silva's 2nd Infantry Division in Villarrica.

During the attack on the Presidential Escort Regiment and the Armed Forces Headquarters complex, the Naval Aviation Esquilo helicopters, each armed with a 7.62mm machine-gun pod and a SBAT 70 rocket-launcher pod, patrolled the area. Esquilo *H-501* was crewed by pilot Lieutenant PAN Benigno Téllez, with mechanic-navigator NCO Oscar Cabral and observers Midshipman Luis Ciancio and

Captain PAN José R. Ocampos Alfaro, Commander of the Naval Aviation, with a Bell H-13H at Sajonia NAS in the late 1970s. (*Almirante* Ret. José R. Ocampos Alfaro)

NCO Rodolfo Rodriguez, while *H-502* was crewed by pilot Captain PAN José Ramón Ocampos Alfaro (the Paraguayan Naval Aviation commander) and mechanic-observer NCO Mario Patiño.

Since the people in Stroessner's bunker had given no indication of surrendering, an ultimatum was issued telling the dictator to stop fighting or the Esquilos would open fire, and Xavante jets would bomb the area with napalm. Fortunately, those in the bunker requested to speak to Rodriguez and the order was cancelled, although once the Air Force was neutralised, a pair of Xavantes took off from Asuncion International Airport with their deadly load and made several low flights over the bunker. One was crewed by 1st Lieutenant PAM Juan Antonio Rojas Duré and Captain PAM Carlos Miguel Woroniecki Quintana, and the other by Captains PAM Gerardo Miguel Angel Maldonado González and Moisés Agustín Paredes Escobar. The actions of the jets was enough to finally convince the dictator and his inner circle that the regime had come to an end.

Commander Carlos Machuca was in charge of the Navy operation, and a force of 250 Marines was organised into three task groups. The commander of the headquarters company was Sub Lieutenant Aldo Gini. They met on 2 February at their base in Sajonia, and set out at 10:00 p.m. for their assigned objectives in several trucks. The first group under Lieutenant Celso Martino, supported by a section of mortars, which was led by Sub Lieutenant Nestor Carrillo, was to attack the Police Headquarters on Plaza Constitución, facing the Congress building and flanked by the Post Office building and Cathedral. After they evacuated some civilians from the area, they took up their positions and started firing at 10:30 p.m. The mortar fire caused severe damage to the building and caused many casualties. An hour later, the firing was suspended and the surrender of the police was demanded over a loud speaker.

The Motorized Police and the Police Fire Brigade surrendered a

Paraguayan Naval Aviation Lt. PAN Benigno A. Tellez. (Author)

few minutes later, but the police force inside the headquarters started firing back again at 11:15 p.m. Ten minutes later, however, a white flag was shown at the entrance of the building. The Marines took

A Naval Aviation Helibras HB-350 Esquilo landing at Sajonia NAS in the late 1980s. (Horacio Decoud)

Navy Marines with a mortar. (*Armada Paraguaya*)

A Navy Marine company. (Author)

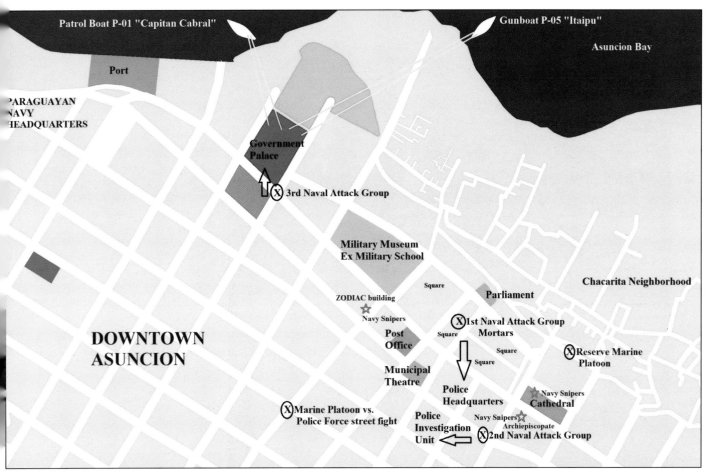

The Navy's attack on the Police Headquarters, the Police Investigation Unit and the Government Palace. (Author)

The Government Palace (left) and the Police Headquarters (right). (Author)

many prisoners, including the Chief of the Police, Lieutenant General Alcibiades Britez Borges. The Navy also placed some snipers on the terrace of a nearby building, called the Zodiac, and in the Cathedral and the Archiepiscopate of Asunción.

The second naval group, led by Sub Lieutenants Edgar Cantero and Blas Noguera, was sent to attack the Police Investigation Unit, at the rear of the Police Headquarters. They encountered no resistance, bursting into the chief Pastor Coronel's office and capturing him. Part of this group, under Lieutenant Samuel Esquivel, with a Marine platoon, was sent to the Chacarita neighbourhood in order to neutralise any paramilitary action led by militants. The third group, led by Lieutenant Jorge Osorio, had been given the objective of occupying the Government Palace. There, a company of the Presidential Escort Regiment led by Major Dos Santos resisted tenaciously. The Marines were supported by naval gunfire from the gunboats *Capitán Cabral*, under Commander Miguel Angel Candia, and *Itaipú* (Commander Gregorio Recalde) in the Bay of Asunción, but they could not take the palace until 4:45 a.m. on 3 February.

A Naval group led by Captain Carlos Cubas also occupied the Channel 9 TV station. A secondary objective was the No. 1 Police Station, which housed the Police NCO School, with 250 personnel. Both of these tasks were accomplished without firing a single bullet. Meanwhile, there was a fierce confrontation in central Asunción between the Marines and members of the Police Special Forces who were in a truck, which was destroyed by fire from the Marines, causing numerous fatalities. After the neutralising of the Police Force, the

The Paraguayan Navy patrol boat P-01 *Capitán Cabral*. (Author)

The Paraguayan Navy gunboat P-05 *Itaipú* with a Naval Aviation Esquilo helicopter about to land in the rear deck. (Horacio Decoud)

A Police Special Force truck after it was attacked by a Marine platoon in downtown Asunción (*Diario Hoy*)

A Marine inspecting a military truck of the Presidential Escort Regiment damaged by combat near the Government Palace. (*Diario Hoy*)

The day after the coup, Marines guarding the Police Headquarters in downtown Asunción. (*Diarios Ultima Hora*)

Navy had 500 prisoners guarded by 90 Marines. The rest of the force was sent to join the attack on the Presidential Escort Regiment.

In Puerto Presidente Stroessner, a naval force led by Captain Amado Rodriguez, including a lieutenant, eight NCOs and 20 sailors, captured Mario Abdo Benitez, the private secretary of General Stroessner, and some local politicians. Meanwhile, the Frontier Battalion commander, a Colonel Dominguez, who was loyal to Stroessner, sent 20 soldiers under Lieutenant Llanes to fight the Navy forces, but when they arrived, Captain Rodriguez ordered the attacking troops to retreat under the threat of being fired upon. Wisely, the Army troops returned to their base in order to avoid a bloody confrontation.

On the other side of the uprising, Colonel Regis Romero's troops – no more than 240 well-equipped soldiers, 20 NCOs and officers, supported by five *Cascavel* armoured vehicles – headed to the Paraguayan Air Force main base in Ñu-Guazú. Romero knew that the commander of the Paratrooper Regiment, Colonel Eduardo Sosa, would remain neutral.

By the time they reached the Air Force base, they learned that a fellow conspirator, Air Force Colonel Hugo Escobar Anzoategui, and approximately 70 high-ranking officers of the FAP had already taken over the site. Captain PAM Victor Insfrán, who was Lieutenant General Andrés Rodriguez's pilot and also the commander of the Helicopter Air Group (GAH) in the FAP, had a pair of Esquilos armed with machine-gun and rocket launcher pods to support the uprising. Initially the situation with the FAP was unknown and the Cascavel armoured vehicles fired several shots at the command

A Marine and an Infantry soldier downtown Asunción. (*ABC Color*)

The Paraguayan Air Force main base in the city of Luque. Asunción International Airport is visible in the background. (Author)

From left to right: Brig. Gen. Alcibiades Soto Valleau, Commander of the FAP; Col. Marino Ruiz Alonso, Commander of the Tactical Air Group (GAT), and Colonel Dionisio Cabello Amarilla, who became the new Commander of the FAP after the coup. (FAP)

Years before the coup, the then Major Hugo Escobar Anzoategui (right) greeting President General Stroessner (left). (Hugo Escobar A.)

building and the car of Colonel Marino Ruiz Alonso, the Tactical Air Group commander, but he escaped unhurt. The Cascavel vehicles were deployed at strategic points within the Air Force base in case it was attacked by artillery forces, but this never happened. The FAP commander, Brigadier General Alcibiades Soto, was not at the base; he was attending a social gathering outside Asunción. Learning about the events that were taking place involving his unit, he quickly tried to return in order to organize a counterattack with the Xavantes, Tucanos and even the ancient T-6Ds.

Upon his arrival at Ñu-Guazú, after trying unsuccessfully to exert his authority, the commander was persuaded to surrender by Colonels Romero and Escobar, with the aid of 150 troops. He was taken to the Cavalry base as a prisoner. Air Force Colonels Carlos Giménez and Dionisio Cabello, and Majors Porfirio Figari and Ramón Astigarraga were sent to the Tactical Air Group (GAT) to officially take control of the unit and the *Líneas Aéreas Paraguayas* (LAP) installations. Colonel César Aguilera did the same with the Military Air Transport (TAM), as did Lieutenant Colonel Aurelio Duarte with the LATN (*Líneas Aéreas de Transporte Nacional*) installations. Air Force Majors Rogelio Sanabria and Hugo Martínez were appointed to be in charge of Asunción International Airport security. Captain PAM Victor

A group of FAP First Fighter Squadron pilots at the Tactical Air Group (GAT) base at Asunción International Airport in the late 1980s. (FAP)

Two FAP pilots aboard an AT-27 Tucano of the Special Aerial Operation Squadron. (FAP)

FAP Paratroop Regiment in a parade in the 1970s. (FAP)

A paratroop platoon getting ready for a jump from a TAM Douglas C-47 in the early 1980s. (FAP)

An armed FAP Xavante jet. (FAP)

A pair of FAP EMB.312/AT-27 Tucanos in flight. (Michel Anciaux)

Insfrán remained in the Cavalry Headquarters with an armed Esquilo helicopter.

As previously mentioned, Brigadier General Eumelio Bernal, the 1st Infantry Division commander, was in charge of neutralising the Engineering Corps, Signal Corps and Police Special Force Unit (FOPE), and eventually taking over the national telephone company ANTELCO. When he was about to start his move, two senior officers from the Signal Corps, Colonels Ramón Esquivel and José Tomás Centurión, presented themselves at his headquarters and declared their support for the coup. Bernal ordered them to seize ANTELCO, which they did without resistance. The Signal Corps commander, General Vicente Flor, also supported the conspirators, and while General Alejandro Schreiber, the Engineering Corps commander, remained loyal to Stroessner, he surrendered to Bernal in the early morning of 3 February when he heard of the course of events. Colonel Galo Escobar, commander of the FOPE, also supported the uprising, but since he arrived late at his unit, a truck full of his men headed for the Police Headquarters but were neutralised by the Marines in

The Presidential Escort Regiment headquarters the day after the coup. (*El Diario Noticias*)

Three FAP Embraer EMB-312/AT-27 Tucano with gun pods and rocket launcher pods. (Col. Roberto Idoyaga)

Two Cavalry officers, 1st Lt. Alfredo Florenciañez Gibbons (left) and Sub-Lt. Pablo Quintana (right) posing happily next to a Cascavel the day after the coup. (*El Diario Noticias*)

A Cascavel multirole armoured vehicle of the Cavalry, day after the coup. (*El Diario Noticias*)

Cavalry Urutú armoured personnel carriers the day after the coup. (*El Diario Noticias & Diario Hoy*)

downtown Asunción.

Meanwhile, in the bunker at the Armed Forces Headquarters complex, Stroessner decided to talk to Rodriguez in order to stop the butchery. Lieutenant General Alejandro Fretes Dávalos, the Army Chief of Staff, telephoned Rodriguez, who first of all demanded the immediate surrender of Stroessner. Fretes Dávalos requested to talk to him personally, so he was brought to the Cavalry Headquarters in an ambulance. After a brief conversation, Fretes Dávalos talked to Gustavo Stroessner on the phone, telling him that nothing else was possible and any further resistance would be useless. It was only then that everybody in the bunker decided to surrender. When Rodriguez learned about this he ordered a ceasefire. At 12:40 a.m. on 3 February, those in the bunker filed out one by one, led by General Stroessner. Colonel Lino C. Oviedo received them and told Stroessner that he had orders to take him to the Cavalry Headquarters. Stroessner told him that he was tired and wanted to go home to sleep, but Rodriguez insisted and said he would place him in his own house. The convoy that took Stroessner to the Cavalry Headquarters was composed of a leading jeep, an Urutú armoured vehicle which carried the generals and colonels who were with Stroessner in the bunker, a black Chevrolet Caprice carrying General Stroessner, Colonel Gustavo Stroessner and his wife, Graciela Stroessner, Colonel Lino Oviedo and the driver, and a pair of Cascavel armoured vehicles behind. During this short trip, Stroessner said that the coup was not necessary because he would

Cavalry troops the day after the coup. (*El Diario Noticias*)

THE 1989 COUP D'ETAT IN PARAGUAY: THE END OF A LONG DICTATORSHIP, 1954–1989

Collateral damage. One of the houses at the rear of the Presidential Escort Regiment base severely affected by mortar fire. (*Diario Hoy*)

A damaged building near the battle zone; fortunately, civilians were evacuated before the fighting began. (*Diario Hoy*)

The former President of Paraguay, General of the Army Alfredo Stroessner, climbing the stairs to board the LAP 707-321B that would carry him into exile. (*El Diario Noticias*)

"By this document I present my irrevocable resignation to the position of President of the Republic of Paraguay and that of Commander-in-Chief of its Armed Forces. General of the Army Alfredo Stroessner"

LAP Boeing 707-321B reg. ZP-CCE with the ex-President Stroessner taking off from Asunción International Airport on 5 February 1989 to Campinas, Brazil. (Patrick Laureau)

have resigned in a few years, but Oviedo ordered him to shut up! Once in the Cavalry base, the head of the uprising refused to meet the once powerful dictator.

The situation regarding the Artillery branch, whose base was in the city of Paraguarí, was confusing. There were insistent rumours that it was going to maintain its support for Stroessner, but nothing happened on 2 February. The conspirators were busy fighting to secure the capital, but once the situation was under control, Rodriguez planned to send a column of tanks supported by three armed Esquilo helicopters of the FAP to check the situation with the Artillery. First, he ordered two Tucanos of the FAP to fly over Paraguarí early in the morning of 3 February to check the situation, but nothing unusual was noticed and no further actions were taken. Two days later, Artillery commander Colonel Tomás Aquino and some of his officers visited Lieutenant General Rodriguez to deny any support for Stroessner's regime.

The Final Outcome

The total number of military forces mobilised for the uprising was around 2,000. At that time, the Paraguayan Armed Forces had approximately 23,000 effectives, with 18,000 in the Army, 3,000 in the Navy and 2,000 in the Air Force. The Police force had almost 10,000 effectives. Although official reports showed very few casualties – 31 fatalities (two civilians, a Cavalry officer, 21 REP privates, two police officers and five police NCOs) and 58 wounded military and police personnel – the estimated number was actually around 170 lives lost, mostly in the Presidential Escort Regiment.

It was Lieutenant General Rodriguez's intention to install Dr Luis Maria Argaña, one of the most prominent leaders of the traditionalists in the Colorado Party, as provisional president, but that idea was not accepted by members of the military high command, who wanted Rodriguez himself to be in the presidency.

Meanwhile, Stroessner and his family were unwanted guests of the Cavalry, and of the country as a whole. For a real and deep pacification of the country, he had to leave Paraguay and go into exile, but the problem was where to send him. It was initially thought to send him far from Paraguay, to either the US or Europe, but neither the American nor many European governments would agree to receive him. Chile and South Africa also refused his presence, so Rodriguez convinced the Brazilian Government, through its ambassador in Paraguay, Manoel Soares Carbonar, to provide a place of exile.

Once an agreement was reached, Rodriguez ordered General Calvet, the general manager of *Líneas Aéreas Paraguayas* (LAP), to prepare a jet and its crew for a flight to Brazil. He also ordered Calvet to be the pilot of that flight, but he refused, so another crew was chosen, comprising pilot Colonel Darío Maciel, co-pilot Lieutenant Colonel Eligio Lezcano, Major Andrés Duarte (second co-pilot), NCO Alberto Ayala (flight engineer), NCO Miguel León (second flight engineer) and Ralf Gehre, Lilian Segovia, Patricia Sekatcheff and Adriana Ayub (flight attendants). The aircraft was LAP's Boeing 707-321B, with the civil registration ZP-CCE. On the afternoon of 5 February, Stroessner, his family and other ex-members of his regime – 30 people in all – were taken to the presidential area of Asunción International Airport under military guard, where they boarded the jet to take them into exile. The aircraft took off at 5:50 p.m. and landed at Viracopos Airport near São Paulo after two hours. Stroessner and family first lived in Itumbiara, but then moved to the coast, to Guaratuba, and finally to the capital, Brasilia. He never returned to Paraguay, eventually dying in Brasilia at the age of 93 on 16 August 2006. He had been suffering from pneumonia after undergoing a hernia operation, but the immediate cause of his death was a stroke.

In the days following the coup, the Congress was dissolved and several leading officials of Stroessner's regime were arrested, especially members of the militant group of the Colorado Party and ex-ministers. High-ranking military officers who remained loyal to the dictator were arrested and held for a few days in the Cavalry's main base, and later transferred to the Army Recruiting Headquarters for a few months. At the end of 1989, all were officially sent into retirement.

4

THE AFTERMATH

A new president after 35 years

Lieutenant General Andrés Rodriguez became provisional President of Paraguay in a ceremony that took place in the Government Palace on the afternoon of 3 February 1989. Later the same day, Dr Juan Ramón Chaves was once again appointed as president of the Colorado Party. In the following days, all commanders of the Armed Forces were changed, as well as ministers, presidents and directors of public companies. Among the "new faces" were the following:
- Minister of Defence: Lieutenant General Adolfo Samaniego
- Minister of Health: Dr Juan Manuel Cano
- Minister of Public Works and Communication: Lieutenant General (ret.) Porfirio Pereira Ruiz Díaz, ex-Mayor of Asunción
- Minister of Justice and Labour: Dr Alexis Frutos Vaesken
- Minister of the Interior: Lieutenant General Orlando Machuca Vargas
- Minister of Foreign Affairs: Dr Luis Maria Argaña
- Minister of Agriculture and Livestock: Agricultural engineer Hernando Bertoni, the only minister of the Stroessner regime that was confirmed in the new government
- Minister of the Treasury: Civil engineer Enzo Debernardi
- Minister of Industry and Commerce: Dr Antonio Zuccolillo
- Minister of Education: Prof Dr Dionisio Gonzalez Torres
- Supreme Court of Justice: Dr Alberto Correa (President) and the following members: Dr Benito Pereira Saguier, Dr Humberto Garcete Lamblasse, Dr Justo Pucheta Ortega and Dr Carlos Pussineri Oddone
- *Líneas Aéreas Paraguayas* (LAP) president: Air Force Colonel Dionisio Cabello Amarilla. The general manager was Air Force Colonel César Rafael Cramer Espinola, who was also a captain in LAP
- Military Air Transport (TAM) commander: Air Force Colonel César Aguilera Torres
- Líneas Aéreas de Transporte Nacional (LATN) commander: Air Force Lieutenant Colonel Rogelio Sanabria
- Paraguayan Merchant Navy (FLOMERES) commander: Navy Captain Anibal Gino Pertile

President Andrés Rodriguez Pedotti. (*Enciclopedia Hispana*)

- Paraguayan Navy commander: Vice Admiral Eduardo Gonzalez Petit
- Army Training School commander: Brigadier General Abraham Abed
- Army War School commander: Brigdier General Otello Carpinelli Yegros
- Army Chief of Staff: Brigadier General Eumelio Bernal Jimenez
- I Army Corps commander: Brigadier General Ramón Humberto Garcete
- II Army Corps commander: Brigadier General Ramón Bogado Silva
- III Army Corps commander: Brigadier General Juan de Dios Garbett
- Army Combat Support commander: Brigadier General Juan Manuel Campos Guillén
- Army Logistics commander: Brigadier General Victor Aguilera Torres
- Paraguayan Air Force commander: Colonel Dionisio Cabello Amarilla (promoted to brigadier general Later that year)
- Army Presidential Attaché: Colonel Anibal Regis Romero (promoted to brigadier general later that year)
- Police commander: Brigadier General Francisco Sanchez
- Mayor of Asunción: Colonel (ret.) José Luis Adler Ibañez

President Rodriguez called for new elections within 90 days, which would take place on 1 May that year. He immediately restored press liberties and freedom of speech, freed political prisoners and welcomed home exiles.

The name of the dictator began to be removed from around Paraguay: Puerto President Stroessner became Ciudad del Este (East City); Asunción International Airport's terminal changed its name from "*Presidente Stroessner*" to "*Silvio Pettirossi*", who was the first Paraguayan pilot; and a huge statue of Stroessner on top of Lambaré

Asunción International Airport main passenger terminal building, in the 1980s (top) with the name "*Presidente Stroessner*", and in the 1990s (bottom) as "*Silvio Pettirossi*". (Author)

A huge statue of Stroessner being removed from a monument on top of Lambaré Hill. (*ABC Color*)

Table 13: May 1989 Election Results			
Candidate	Political Party	Votes	Percentage
Andrés Rodriguez Pedotti	*Partido Colorado* (ANR)	882,957	76.59
Domingo I. Laino Figueredo	*Partido Liberal Radical Autentico* (PLRA)	241,829	20.98
Fernando Vera Sánchez	*Partido Revolucionario Febrerista* (PRF)	11,007	0.95
Secundino Nuñez Medina	*Partido Demócrata Cristiano* (PDC)	8,032	0.70
Carlos Ferreira Ibarra	*Partido Liberal* (PL)	4,423	0.38
Blas Manuel Mangabeira	*Partido Liberal Radical* (PLR)	3,545	0.31
Carlos Gustavo Callizo Parini	*Partido Humanista* (PH)	1,058	0.09
Blank/null votes		11,197	-
TOTAL		1,164,048	100
Registered voters/participation		2,226,061	53.29
Source: Electoral Justice Tribunal			

Hill was demolished in the early 1990s. Since then, bronze plates with his name have been removed from squares, streets, institutions, buildings, etc, although some of them do still exist.

First Democratic Elections in 35 years

General elections took place on 1 May 1989. The population of Paraguay had reached 4,103,909, of whom 2,226,061 were registered to vote. Seven political parties participated, and the results were as shown in Table 13.

The only opposition party that did not participate in the elections was the Paraguayan Communist Party (PCP), which was still banned, but it was legalised later that year. Andrés Rodriguez and the Colorado Party were the clear winners in the elections. The distribution of the 72 seats for the Chamber of Representatives in the Congress was 48 for the ANR, 21 for the PLRA, two for the PRF and one for the PLR.

Rodriguez was the last active military man to be President of Paraguay. As has been mentioned, he only served in office from 1988-93, and immediately following the 1993 elections he transferred power to a civilian, Juan Carlos Wasmosy Monti, also from the ANR, to serve until 1998. He was succeeded by Raul Cubas Grau (ANR) for the 1998-2003 term, but he resigned on 28 March 1999, being substituted by the head of the Legislative Power, Senator Luis Angel Gonzalez Macchi (ANR), who completed the term. Nicanor Duarte Frutos (ANR) was elected for the 2003-08 term, then for 2008-13, the ex-Catholic bishop Fernando Lugo Mendez (PDC) was head of state, but was impeached and forced to resign by the Parliament on 22 June 2012. Lugo's vice-president, Dr Luis Federico Franco Gomez (PLRA), completed the term. In 2013, Horacio Manuel Cartes Jara (ANR) was elected president for the 2013-18 term. Finally, in 2018, Mario Abdo Benitez Jr. (ANR), incredibly the son of Stroessner's private secretary, won the Presidential elections for the 2018-2023 term.

A few months after the coup, President Rodriguez (sixth from the left) and all the "Carlos" and "Victor" commanders. (Roberto Paredes)

CONCLUSION

The year 1989 marked a milestone in the history of Paraguay. By then, the political model implanted by General Stroessner was archaic; the last surviving dictatorship in South America was, in the words of renowned Paraguayan writer Augusto Roa Bastos, "an island surrounded by democracy". Although the cause of the coup could have been the personal motivations of those involved, the model of government that had prevailed for 35 years no longer worked and was about to collapse. Rodriguez took advantage of these circumstances to organise and carry out the coup that finally ended the dictatorship in Paraguay. His economic interests were saved, although he could not enjoy them for long as he died just eight years after the coup, but the country gained a great deal with public liberties, the release of many political prisoners and the return of many exiles. Since then, to this day, democratically elected governments have succeeded.

Years after the coup, the event became known as the "Coup of the Candlemas" (*Golpe de la Candelaria*) in honour to the Catholic festival of the Virgin of the Candlemas, which is celebrated on 2 February.

Regarding the violation of human rights, during Stroessner's regime some 20,090 people were direct victims: a total of 19,862 were arrested arbitrarily or illegally, and 18,772 of these were tortured; 59 were executed extra judicially and 336 more are missing; 3,470 were sent into exile. If the family members of those victims are also considered, there were 107,987 indirect victims.

SOURCES

Arce Farina, José Arce, *Las Fuerzas Armadas y el Stronismo*. Colección 60 años del Stronismo. (Asunción, Editorial El Lector, 2014; ISBN 9-789995-314590).

Benitez, Luis G., *31 Años de Paz y Progreso, 1943-1985*. (Asunción, 1985).

Camazano Alamino, Aparecido & Rudnei Dias Da Cunha, *Embraer 326GB Xavante AT-26. Aeronaves Militares Brasileiras – 1*. (Porto Alegre, Mala Direta Serviços Graficos, 2000).

Diario Última Hora, *La noche que cambió la historia*. (Asunción, Correo Semanal. Sábado 11 de febrero de 1989).

Diario Crónica, *Tronó el cañón y la libertad dio un paso al frente*. (Asunción, Viernes 10 de Febrero de 1989).

Diario Hoy, "El Gral. Stroessner se ha rendido…" (Asunción, Viernes 3 de Febrero de 1989).

Diario Última Hora, *Un golpe militar derrocó a Stroessner*. (Asunción, Viernes 3 de Febrero de 1989).

El Diario Noticias, *Se fue Stroessner*. (Asunción, Lunes 6 de Febrero de 1989).

El Diario Noticias, *El Golpe*. Edición Especial. (Asunción, Sábado 3 de Febrero de 1990).

El Diario Noticias, *1989. El año del cambio*. (Asunción, Anuario, 1989).

El Diario Revista, *Aquel 2 de Febrero*. (Asunción, Domingo 12 de Febrero de 1989).

El Diario Revista, *Las Conversaciones bajo el fuego. El Golpe en la mira*. (Asunción, Domingo 26 de Febrero de 1989)

English, Adrian J., *Revolutions, Civil War and Coups D'État. Internal Disturbances in Paraguay during the 20th Century*. (Nottingham, Caliver Books/Partizan Press, 2011; ISBN 978-1-85818-622-1).

English, Adrian J., *An Outline History of the Paraguayan Army*. (Article published on 31 January 2007 at www.histarmar.com.ar)

Fariña, Bernardo Neri & Alfredo Boccia Paz, *El Paraguay bajo el Stronismo*. (Asunción, Editorial El Lector, 2010).

Farina, Bernardo Neri, *El Último Supremo*. (Asunción, Editorial El Lector, 2003; ISBN 9-789995-312602).

Flores Jr., Jackson, *Aeronaves Militares Brasileiras 1916-2015*. (Rio de Janeiro, Action Editora, 2015; ISBN 9-788585-654412).

Frutos Neusffamer, Cristóbal Alberto, *Album de Oro de la Segunda Grandeza Nacional. Stroessner*. Volumen 1 & 2. (Asunción, 1979 and 1985).

González Delvalle, Alcibíades, *El Golpe del 3 de Febrero de 1989*. Colección Guerras y Violencia Política en el Paraguay. Tomo 17. (Asunción, Editorial El Lector, 2013; ISBN 9-789995-313555).

González Delvalle, Alcibíades, *Yo, Alfredo Stroessner*. Colección Protagonistas de la Historia. (Asunción, Editorial El Lector, 2011; ISBN 9-789995-317423).

Higuchi, Helio, Reginaldo Bacchi & Paulo Roberto Bastos Jr., *O Stuart no Brasil. M3/M3A1 e derivados*. Biblioteca Tecnología & Defesa. (Sao Paulo, Tecnodefesa Editorial Ltda, 2015; ISBN 9-788569-997009).

Lachi, Marcelo, *Insurgentes. La resistencia armada a la dictadura de Stroessner*. (Asunción, Editorial Arandurá, 2004; ISBN 99925-45-65-1).

Legal, María Estela, *Mi vida con el Presidente Alfredo Stroessner*. (Asunción, Editorial Medusa, 2008; ISBN 9-789995-385118).

Miranda, Anibal, *Stroessner*. (Asunción, Ediciones del diario Ultima Hora, 2004; ISBN 99925-3-307-2).

Miranda, Aníbal, *Crimen Organizado en Paraguay*. (Asunción, Editorial Miranda & Asociados, 2001; ISBN 99925-4-163-0).

Mora, Frank O. & Jerry W. Cooney, *El Paraguay y Estados Unidos*. (Asunción, Intercontinental Editora, 2009; ISBN 9-789995-334994).

Nickson, Andrew, *La Guerra Fría y el Paraguay*. Colección 60 años del Stronismo. (Asunción, Editorial El Lector, 2014; ISBN 9-789995-314507).

Nickson, Andrew, *Las Guerrillas del Alto Paraná*. Colección Guerras y Violencia Política en el Paraguay. Tomo 16. (Asunción, Editorial El Lector, 2013; ISBN 9-789995-313548).

Ortiz Granada, Miguel A., *Un Museo del Golpe*. (Asunción, Revista El Diario Noticias. Domingo 9 de Diciembre de 1990).

Paredes, Roberto, Ricardo Benítez Rolandi & David Vargas, *"Los Carlos"*. Capitulo 19. Enciclopedia Histórica del Paraguay. Episodios y Anécdotas. (Asunción, Diario La Nación. Editorial Gráfica Intersudamericana, 1998).

Roberto Paredes y Liz Varela, *Los Carlos. Historia del derrocamiento de Alfredo Stroessner*. (Asunción, Editorial Servilibro, 2005).

Paredes, Roberto, *Stroessner y el Stronismo*. (Asunción, Diario Última Hora, 2004).

Paredes, Roberto, *Post-Stronismo: Luces y Sombras*. (Asunción, Diario Última Hora, 2005).

Paredes, Roberto, *El Golpe que derrocó a Stroessner*. (Asunción, Editorial Servilibro, 2011; ISBN 9-789995-302733).

Rivarola, Milda, *La Resistencia Armada al Stronismo*. Colección 60 años del Stronismo. (Asunción, Editorial El Lector, 2014; ISBN 9-789995-314545).

Ruiz Alonso, Coronel (SR) Marino, *Lealtades, Traiciones y Mentiras. Memorias y Reflexiones del Comandante de los Xavantes en la noche del Golpe de la Candelaria*. (Asunción, Edición del autor, 2016).

Sapienza Fracchia, Antonio Luis, *La Historia de Líneas Aéreas Paraguayas*. (Asunción, Edición del autor, 2004).

Sapienza Fracchia, Antonio Luis, *Historia Gráfica de la Fuerza Aérea Paraguaya, 1913-2013*. (Luque, Fuerza Aérea Paraguaya, 2013).

Sapienza Fracchia, Antonio Luis, *The Chaco Air War. The First Modern Air War in Latin America, 1932-1935*. (Solihull, Helion & Co. Ltd. 2018; ISBN 978-1-911512-96-7).

Sigal Fogliani, Ricardo, *Blindados Argentinos, de Uruguay y Paraguay*. (Buenos Aires, Ayer y Hoy Ediciones, 1997).

Vittone, Coronel DEM (SR) Luis, *Paraguay, Pasado de Gloria, Presente de Grandeza*. (Asunción, Industria Grafica Comuneros S.A., 1981).

Zeitoun Moralez, João Paulo, *EMB-312 Tucano. Brazil's turboprop success story*. (Texas, Harpia Publishing. Houston, 2017; ISBN 978-0-9973092-3-2).

ACKNOWLEDGEMENTS

The author is deeply thankful to Adrian J. English, Tito Aranda, Michel Anciaux, Lilian Segovia, Carlos Corvalán, Horacio Decoud, Renato Angulo, Dra. Magdalena Cubas, the late Admiral (ret.) José Ramón Ocampos Alfaro, Navy Captains Luis Mariano Ciancio Petters and Luis Amilcar Vera Ferreira, the ex-FAP commander Brigadier General (ret.) Alcibiades Soto Valleau, the ex-FAP commander Brigadier General (ret.) Dionisio Cabello Amarilla, FAP Colonel (ret.) Marino Ruiz Alonso, FAP Colonel Carlos Melgarejo, FAP Colonel Roberto Ydoyaga, the Paraguayan Navy and Naval Aviation, the Paraguayan Army, the Paraguayan Air Force, *Instituto de Historia Museo Militar del Ministerio de Defensa*, The Roosevelt Library of the CCPA, *Diario ABC Color* and *Diario Ultima Hora*, among others, for their invaluable help.

ABOUT THE AUTHOR

Antonio Luis Sapienza Fracchia was born in Asunción, Paraguay on 14th May 1960. He graduated from the *Catholic University of Asunción* where he got a B.A. in Clinical Psychology. He also took specialized English courses at Tulane University of New Orleans, Louisiana, USA and San Diego State University in California. He is at present an English Teacher and one of the Academic Coordinators at the Centro Cultural Paraguayo-Americano (CCPA), a binational institute in Asunción. Married with two children, he resides in the capital.

He is an Aviation Historian and a founding member of the *Instituto Paraguayo de Historia Aeronáutica "Silvio Pettirossi"*. He is also a corresponding member of similar institutes and academies in Argentina, Bolivia, Chile, Colombia, Spain, the United States and Uruguay. He has written more than 600 articles in specialized magazines and web pages on the Paraguayan Aviation history, and has given numerous lectures in schools, universities, institutes, military and civil institutions in Paraguay and abroad. Since 2010, he has been an aviation history professor in the Paraguayan Air Force (FAP) and has received a total of five decorations for his academic merits, one from Brazil, two from Argentina and two from Paraguay. He has published thirteen books, and this is his third book with Helion.